MW00444009

iACTUATE

100 days of Inspiration
Volume One

iACTUATE

100 days of Inspiration
Volume One

'Sheg'
Olusegun Aranmolate

Inspivia Books
P.O. Box 331891
Nashville, TN, 37203
www.inspiviabooks.com

The information presented in this book is not in anyway meant to substitute the valuable advice of your health-care professional. It is advisable that you consult with your doctor about matters that concern your health or require medical attention, and before embarking on any form of treatment, diet, or exercise.

iACTUATE: 100 days of Inspiration, Volume One.
© Copyright 2008 by Inspivia Books.

Chief Editor – Daniel Smyth
Associate Editor – Karlene Roberts
Cover Designer – Joshua Rhodes
Author Photographer – Tony Denning
Book Design – Inspivia Design

All rights reversed. No part of this book can be used or reproduced, in part or in whole, by any means, by anyone, without written permission from Olusegun Aranmolate or Inspivia Books. For permission to reproduce the information in this book for commercial purposes or redistribution, please e-mail: copyright@iactuate.com.

To contact the author, Olusegun 'Sheg' Aranmolate:
sheg@iactuate.com

ISBN-10: 0615193846
ISBN-13: 978-0615193847

This Inspivia Books Paperback Edition May 2008.
Inspivia Books is a trademark of Inspivia, Inc.

Printed in the United States of America

For more information about this book, please check the book website:
www.iactuate.com

table of contents:

dedication:

I dedicate this book to my parents, Dr. Olusegun and Mrs. Adenike Aranmolate, who instilled in me great morals and values, and to my little lady, Nilaja C. Aranmolate, who truly inspired me to follow my dreams.

I am Thankful.

acknowledgment:

First and foremost, I thank the Almighty for giving me the strength and knowledge to write such a great book. I thank my family and friends for their encouragement, support, and efforts in helping me make this book a reality. I thank my friend and art director, Joshua Rhodes, for all the time and effort he put into designing the perfect book cover. I thank my friend and fellow author, Terri Rowland, for proofreading the book. I thank my friend and associate editor, Karlene Roberts, for editing and proofreading the book. Finally, I thank my good friend and chief editor, Daniel J. Smyth, for all his helpful comments and criticisms.

I am Grateful.

foreword:
The Good Will
Immanuel Kant (1724-1804)

It is impossible to conceive anything at all in the world, or even out of it, which can be taken as good without qualification, except a **good will**. Intelligence, wit, judgement, and any other *talents* of the mind we may care to name, or courage, resolution, and constancy of purpose, as qualities of *temperament*, are without doubt good and desirable in many respects; but they can also be extremely bad and hurtful when the will is not good which has to make use of these gifts of nature, and which for this reason has the term "*character*" applied to its peculiar quality. It is exactly the same with "*gifts of fortune.*" Power, wealth, honour, even health and that complete well-being and contentment with one's state which goes by the name of "happiness," produce boldness, and as consequence often overboldness, as well, unless a good will is present by which their influence on the mind—and so too the whole principle of action—may be corrected and adjusted to universal ends; not to mention that rational and impartial spectator can never feel approval in contemplating the uninterrupted prosperity of a being graced by no touch of a pure and good will, and that consequently a good will seems to constitute the indispensable condition of our very worthiness to be happy.......

"**Immanuel Kant** (1724-1804) is considered one of the most important philosophers of the Western World."
Excerpt from Groundwork of the Metaphysic of Morals.
Translated by H.J. Paton.
Copyrighted by Hutchinson Publishing Group Limited.

introduction:

When I started writing this book, every time I told people about my writing ambitions, it was almost inevitable that I wasn't asked for the title or the overarching idea of the book. Like many authors, however, I started the book without a title and had to confess as such. Nevertheless, I always told my inquirers that I was writing a book to **actuate** people to improve their lives. Interestingly, every time I talked about my book, I always emphasized the words "i" and "ACTUATE," so I eventually concluded that "iACTUATE" would be a great book title. This wasn't necessarily due to the convenience of saying the title, but rather because the title encompasses my entire ideology behind the book. The lowercase "i" represents my humble self and the capitalized "ACTUATE" represents my intense desire to incite, motivate, and inspire myself and others to succeed in life.

Over the course of my young life, I have learned a lot about life, justice, ethics, and morality from my brilliant parents and by reading the works of some of the world's greatest thinkers, such as Aristotle, Immanuel Kant, Friedrich Nietzsche, Karl Marx, Albert Einstein, and Wole Soyinka. However, I believe that my personal life experiences in Africa and around the world have been my greatest instructor of all. Drawing from all I've learned, I wrote this book to truly inspire people, regardless of their age, creed, or gender and show them that we still live in a world filled with compassion and inspiration. I hope the time my readers spend reading this book will be a journey for them to better understand their strengths and weaknesses and to realize that they are living sources of inspiration. I hope that, in reading all my messages and performing all the simple mental and physical activities in the book, my readers will grow physically, mentally, and emotionally, and will develop their own unique philosophies of life so that they also can become ambassadors of goodwill to all.

Thanks,

Olusegun Aranmolate

notes from author:
about the book

I want to thank my readers for reading or attempting to read this wonderful book, iACTUATE: 100 days of Inspiration, which I wrote with the sole purpose of inspiring people to improve themselves mentally, physically, emotionally, and even spiritually. In this book, I provide my readers with one-hundred simple passages that will provide them with logical reasons to be inspired.

This book was written to be a daily devotional for one-hundred (100) days, with each day representing a new message and new set of daily activities. However, I understand that we live in a busy world and many of us may be tempted to read the entire book all at once. iACTUATE can indeed be read all at once, but I strongly urge you to reread the messages on a daily basis, complete the several physical and mental activities in the book, and write down your daily reflections. All this will help you develop and improve your overall being. I strongly hope that my readers will be able to write their messages so that they can inspire other people in the world.

notes from author:
how to use the book

Each day in iACTUATE: 100 days of Inspiration is divided into two main sections, namely the message and schema.

1. **message:**
The message section provides the readers with an inspirational passage each day.

2. **schema:**
The schema (plan) section is interactive and provides readers with daily mental and physical activities. It has four major parts, including the following:

a. **body:**
This consists of simple, daily physical activities that strengthen the body. To fully benefit from this section of the book, you have to be familiar with the following exercises:

☐ jogging		☐ standing rows	
☐ sit-ups		☐ lunges	
☐ stretching		☐ bench dips	
☐ squats		☐ bicep curls	
☐ lunges		☐ calf-raises	
☐ shoulder presses		☐ push-ups	

b. **mind:**
This consists of two simple mental activities that strengthen the mind and improve our emotions.

c. **goals:**
The goals are meant for readers to write down three activities that they plan to accomplish in the day.

d. **reflections:**
The reflections section leaves a blank area for the readers to write daily reflections that will hopefully inspire someone else someday.

3. *****epoch:**
An epoch is a new beginning or era, and I believe that, after every tens days of reading and using iACTUATE, readers will notice positive improvements and will be entering new eras of their lives. There are ten epochs in this book, each with two isochronal reflections. The isochronal (occurring at equal intervals of time) reflection is a blank area for readers to write down their comments, thoughts, ideas, progress, future aspirations, and even opposing views to my messages.

---

day one:
human potential

> The best and safest thing is to keep a balance in your life, acknowledge the great powers around us and in us. If you can do that, and live that way, you are really a wise man.
> Euripides (484 BC - 406 BC)

A young woman had read some of my inspirational messages on my website and had decided to write me for advice. She wrote me a sincere letter, describing how depressed, confused, and frustrated she was with her life and her family. She said her life was stagnant and it seemed like everyone, except her was succeeding in life. She added, however, that she knew she had the potential to make a difference and change her life but just didn't know where to start. I found her letter touching and it inspired me to help her understand the concept of the "human potential."

The "human potential" is like a corn seed that if planted in the soil is capable of growth. However, if left unattended in the ground, then various elements like disease, pests, weeds, and lack of essential nutrients will have a better chance of diminishing its growth. Every human being has a unique potential to grow and better themselves, but just like the corn seed we need continual attention, nurturing, and care. It is important for us to remove those harmful habits that constantly stunt our growth and to surround ourselves with positive ideas and positive people, similar to pulling weeds and giving a supportive environment for corn seeds to grow. Nevertheless, just as adding excessive fertilizers can be harmful to plants, excessive pressure on ourselves to develop can make us feel worthless and thus tarnish our growth. Simply be good to yourself, detoxify yourself of bad vibes, don't be too critical of yourself, and at the end of the season your potential will reap bountifully.

schema:

body:
- ☐ eat a healthy breakfast.
- ☐ take multivitamins.
- ☐ drink lots of water.
- ☐ stretch several times.
- ☐ take the stairs, instead of the elevator.

mind:
- ☐ visualize a successful day.
- ☐ be kind to everyone.

goals:
- ☐ :
- ☐ :
- ☐ :

reflections:

Olusegun 'Sheg' Aranmolate

day two:
<u>a little kindness</u>

Forget injuries, never forget kindnesses.
Confucius (551 BC - 479 BC)

A few years ago, I was in Nigeria and there was a period of widespread poverty, high unemployment, and food scarcity mainly because corrupt politicians poorly governed the country. It was a devastating period for several families, and I vividly remember that many people were starving, unable to afford healthy meals. Sadly, many merchants and wealthy individuals who had access to stored food supplies began to increase the prices of food items to ensure that they made astronomical gains at the expense of the poor and impoverished. Nevertheless, there were still many generous and kindhearted individuals who offered discounts on food supplies to families and sometimes gave out free food to the famished.

Of course, business thrives on the idea of making a profit for every sale, but during times when human lives are at stake making profits should be the least important issue. In times of despair, when many people are dependent on each other for survival will you be a selfish opportunist, like those merchants who jacked up their prices? Or will you be a selfless philanthropist, striving to share joy and happiness to the less fortunate? Kindness and altruistic behaviors may not always be financially profitable, but these gestures are invaluable to humanity. Become a philanthropist today and change someone's life for the better.

schema:

body:

- ☐ eat a healthy breakfast.
- ☐ take multivitamins.
- ☐ eat lots of fruits.
- ☐ go for a jog.
- ☐ get a massage.

mind:

- ☐ visualize a successful day.
- ☐ smile and greet everyone.

goals:

- ☐ :
- ☐ :
- ☐ :

reflections:

Olusegun 'Sheg' Aranmolate

day three:
<u>our burden</u>

Judge thyself with the judgment of sincerity, and thou will judge others with the judgment of charity.
John Mitchell Mason (1770 -1829)

Life is filled with its ups and downs, and many of us from a young age have been taught by society to only reveal our successes and triumphs, but to keep secret our failures and problems. As a result, many people today are walking around with many problems that they haven't shared with anyone. I understand that many of us feel that in revealing our problems to others, we might be inconveniencing them or they might lose respect for us as individuals. In fact, however, the reverse is usually true as good people gain respect for us when we share our problems with them—they sincerely empathize and genuinely want to help us lessen our burden.

Hiding our problems is similar to a young boy receiving a bad grade on a report card, and instead of showing it to his parents who could educate him or get him proper help and tutoring, decides to hide it under his pillow. The boy, however, assumes that his parents only want to see good grades and unwisely thinks that because the report card is out of sight, everything is all right. Obviously, his teacher already recorded the bad grade and it will come back to haunt him later in the school year. Don't be like this naïve little boy who failed to reveal his problems to people who could help. If you are having problems in your life, talk to a family member or a friend and if none of them can help, at the very least, seek out a trained professional. Are you going to reveal your problems or are you still going to keep hiding your problems, only to be haunted by them later in life? Do what's right and let someone else help you with your burden.

---

schema:

body:

- ☐ eat a healthy breakfast.
- ☐ take multivitamins.
- ☐ eat lots of yogurt.
- ☐ complete several sit-ups.
- ☐ stretch several times.

mind:

- ☐ laugh at every chance.
- ☐ take a mental vacation.

goals:

- ☐ :
- ☐ :
- ☐ :

reflections:

day four:
<u>mental compartmentalization</u>

When we are planning for posterity, we ought to remember that virtue is not hereditary.
Thomas Paine (1737 – 1809)

Have you ever tried watching two movies on television at the same time—clicking back and forth between both movies? If so, you probably know that it is difficult to fully understand both movies as you miss important parts of the plots. However, you could have avoided wasting your time and ruining your chances of enjoying both movies, if you had watched one movie at a time. Interestingly, this scenario is similar to the way many of us deal with problems in our lives. Instead of "mentally compartmentalizing" our problems, and individually focusing on and solving our problems, we try to multitask and fix all our problems at once—often with little or no success.

Libraries often arrange books on shelves numerically and alphabetically for easy accessibility. Obviously, if libraries randomly placed books on selves without a system, the possibility of finding a book with ease will be unlikely. Likewise, when it comes to sorting and solving our problems, many of us are like unorganized libraries with randomly-scattered books. Consequently, we end up becoming inefficient and disorganized problem solvers. Efficient problem-solving requires us to continually sort our problems so that we are better able to prioritize them and tackle one problem at a time. For this reason, resolve your office issues at work and your household issues at home. Don't try solving both problems at the same time and place.

schema:

body:
- ☐ eat a healthy breakfast.
- ☐ take multivitamins.
- ☐ drink lots of green tea.
- ☐ complete several squats.
- ☐ go for a walk.

mind:
- ☐ meditate.
- ☐ think positively.

goals:
- ☐ :
- ☐ :
- ☐ :

reflections:

Olusegun 'Sheg' Aranmolate

day five:
<u>fear of change</u>

Great ability develops and reveals itself increasingly with every new assignment.
Baltasar Gracian (1601 - 1658)

I remember the first time a friend invited me on a snowboarding trip, and because I grew up in a country devoid of snow, I wanted to ensure that it was a memorable trip. As a result, I began making plans months ahead. I bought a book on snowboarding, read about Salt Lake City, Utah, bought several snowboarding gear, and by the time of the trip I felt prepared to have fun. However, even with all this anticipation, when I got to the mountaintop and saw the large vastness of all the snow below, my excitement turned to fear. I became so scared that I didn't want to snowboard at all. Frankly, do you think that my fears were valid or do you think that I was just a scared loser unable to proceed?

The truth is that many of us, at some point, want to do new things like visit exotic places, live in new cities, or change jobs. But we can easily become apprehensive when given the opportunity to do these things. The initial fear of change is normal because these activities require us to leave our comfort zone and venture into unknown territories. You need to realize that feeling scared of change doesn't make you a coward. In fact, it can make you a more vigilant and heedful person. On the other hand, if you simply succumb to your fears, then you might miss out on great life experiences. When I was on the mountaintop and was about to give up snowboarding, I thought about how much time and energy I had invested in preparing for the trip that I realized that quitting wasn't an option. In such times of apprehension and doubt, remember that you aren't a coward for feeling that way. Nevertheless, you shouldn't let your fears take advantage of you. Go out today and do those things that you have always wanted to do.

schema:

body:
- ☐ eat a healthy breakfast.
- ☐ take multivitamins.
- ☐ eat lots of fresh fish.
- ☐ play with friends and family.
- ☐ get a massage.

mind:
- ☐ appreciate your body.
- ☐ laugh at every chance.

goals:
- ☐ :
- ☐ :
- ☐ :

reflections:

Olusegun 'Sheg' Aranmolate

day six:
the answers within

I can't understand why people are frightened of new ideas. I'm frightened of the old ones.
John Cage (1912 - 1992)

A Greek king gave Archimedes, a great mathematician, the task of determining the quality of a gold crown that the king had recently acquired. This task was difficult for Archimedes because he didn't have any of today's sophisticated tools and techniques to determine the purity of gold. He thought long and hard about all the possible ways to solve his problem, but couldn't devise a viable solution. Resigned to report his failure to the king, Archimedes decided to take a bath before heading to the palace. However, as he submerged himself in the bathwater, he suddenly realized that the buoyancy of water could be used to measure the purity of gold!

The point of this story is that so many of us feel that we have problems too difficult to be fixed and tasks too daunting to be resolved. As a result, we often lose hope. Ironically, as in the case of Archimedes, the solutions to our alleged problems are usually relatively simple. Unlike Archimedes, however, we never discover these solutions because we're not immersed in the right environment, and because we're too distracted to listen to the answers from within ourselves. Next time, you are about to give up on an idea or task because you don't have a solution, take some time off, go to a quiet place, and listen to your inner voice. You might be surprised to find that the solution to your problems is directly in front of you or within you.

schema:

body:
- ☐ eat a healthy breakfast.
- ☐ take multivitamins.
- ☐ eat lots of fruits.
- ☐ go for a jog.
- ☐ complete several lunges.

mind:
- ☐ relax with music.
- ☐ breathe and introspect.

goals:
- ☐ :
- ☐ :
- ☐ :

reflections:

Olusegun 'Sheg' Aranmolate

day seven:
panic attack

Let the fear of danger be a spur to prevent it; he that fears
not, gives advantage to the danger.
    Francis Quarles (1592 - 1644)

The "victim with the keys" is a classic scene that I often see
repeated in several scary and horror movies. This scene usually
depicts scared individuals running away from a killer or a
monster towards a room or a car that represents their freedom
or salvation. Adding to the suspense, these individuals get to the
door, pull out a bunch of keys, and begin to fumble them in
search for the right key. Unfortunately, these already terrified
people then begin to panic, wasting time, as they frantically try
to open the door, only to be captured or hurt by their assailants.

This classic movie scene can be similar to moments in our lives,
especially when we are confronted with physical, financial, or
emotional difficulties. During these times, it usually seems like
every time we get close to our door of salvation, things always
go wrong and we end up getting beaten by our problems.
Interestingly, many of us seem to forget that we have in our
possession, in the form of great ideas, the keys to set ourselves
free—called solutions. However, like those people in the classic
movie scene, we become so overwhelmed that we fail to find
the correct key (solution) from the bunch. Whenever you feel
like you are been pursued by life's problems, and when you
sense that you are close to your door of salvation, don't panic
because anxiety only makes things worse. Instead, try to relax,
take control, find the correct key (solution), and open the door
to your financial, emotional, physical and spiritual freedom.

schema:

body:
- ☐ eat a healthy breakfast.
- ☐ take multivitamins.
- ☐ drink lots of water.
- ☐ complete several push-ups.
- ☐ cook a delicious meal.

mind:
- ☐ plan your future.
- ☐ be kind to everyone.

goals:
- ☐ :
- ☐ :
- ☐ :

reflections:

day eight:
<u>ideal happiness</u>

Happiness depends upon ourselves.
  Aristotle (384 BC - 322 BC)

During my course in life as a personal fitness trainer, I had the opportunity to work with people from various walks of life and to learn the truth that money doesn't always equate to happiness. For example, I remember a wealthy client of mine who owned a business, drove a luxury car, owned a nice home in an expensive neighborhood, and had no problem spending money. However, after working with him and getting to know him, I realized that he was depressed and even suicidal. According to himself, despite all the money at his disposal, he had no reason to love life.

There are many people in the world who are in a similar position as my client. These people are financially successful, and seem to be happy and content with life. Other people see them and wish they had their wonderful lives. Unfortunately, the truth is that many of these people are pretenders who in public seem to have it all, but behind closed doors are living wretched unhappy lives. Be careful of what you wish for in life because you might get it, only for you to realize that it's nothing like what you wanted. Don't wish to be happy like someone else, because we truly never know the entire truth about a person. Instead, gradually develop yourself into a person that embodies and pursues happiness in the right places, such as by helping others, spending time with family and friends, exercising, and in education. Be careful not to think riches will give you happiness or can solve all your problems. If you're not already a happy person, no amount of money in this world can change that fact about you.

schema:

body:
- ☐ eat a healthy breakfast.
- ☐ take multivitamins.
- ☐ eat lots of fresh salad.
- ☐ stretch several times.
- ☐ complete several shoulder presses.

mind:
- ☐ visualize a successful day.
- ☐ be grateful for your life.

goals:
- ☐ :
- ☐ :
- ☐ :

reflections:

day nine:
in denial

No legacy is so rich as honesty.
William Shakespeare (1564 - 1616)

Picture this: you get into your car in the morning on your way to work and as you are driving, you notice that the fuel indicator is blinking, signifying that your car is low on gas. It is very likely that you will be on the lookout for the nearest gas station. Wouldn't it be absurd, if you saw the light blinking and happened to see a gas station ahead, but instead of stopping for gas, you concluded that the light was meaningless because you could smell gasoline in your fuel tank? Obviously, anyone who drives a car knows that this way of thinking is unwarranted and will likely result in the car stalling a few miles down the road.

Denial! There are so many of us who are in denial and are always making excuses to avoid the reality of our problems. Just like the delusional driver who refuses to accept the reality that the car is out of gas, many of us are aware of our problems but continually refuse to accept that fact. We keep making up intelligent and sometimes illogical reasons, why we don't have problems. Nevertheless, we must remember that we are the true judges and the best solvers of our problems—we know them better than anyone else. Therefore, when we make those ridiculous excuses, we're not deceiving anyone but ourselves. You really can't keep on making excuses for your negative actions and keep on ignoring those warning signs because after a few miles down the path of life, you will be stalled and unable to progress any further.

schema:

body:
- ☐ eat a healthy breakfast.
- ☐ take multivitamins.
- ☐ eat lots of yogurt.
- ☐ take the stairs, instead of the elevator.
- ☐ go for a walk.

mind:
- ☐ apologize for your faults.
- ☐ meditate.

goals:
- ☐ :
- ☐ :
- ☐ :

reflections:

Olusegun 'Sheg' Aranmolate

day ten:
<u>fading away</u>

To win without risk is to triumph without glory.
Pierre Corneille (1606 - 1684)

One day, I was in a café, drinking a cup of tea and happened to strike up a conversation with an attractive young woman. We started talking about politics but suddenly started talking about her life. She told me that she used to be a successful fashion model but had recently decided to go back to college to become a teacher. She said she mainly did this out of fear of fading away into oblivion without making a positive difference in the world. Upon hearing her story, I immediately could relate with this woman because every one of us as we mature through life will at some point have the fear or feeling of fading away through time without genuine accomplishments.

The different stages in our lives are similar to the chapters of a book, with each chapter marking a new beginning but a continuation of previous chapters. Just as every chapter in an action novel isn't filled with action sequences, every stage in our lives won't be marked by continuous recognition. There are times when we will be popular and there are times when we will not. There are times when we win and there are times when we fail. Also, there are times when we just need to relax and build up experiences to do those things that really matter to us. It is important to realize that as long as we are breathing, there should be no reason for anyone to be scared of fading away. This fear is only a state of mind—to reverse its effects we need to prove to ourselves that we are not fading away. Go out today and find something that makes you feel good about yourself. Remember the world is filled with endless possibilities and the limit of your sky is dependent on how high you are willing to fly.

schema:

body:
- ☐ eat a healthy breakfast.
- ☐ take multivitamins.
- ☐ eat lots of fresh fish.
- ☐ stretch several times.
- ☐ complete several push-ups.

mind:
- ☐ meditate.
- ☐ smile and greet everyone.

goals:
- ☐ :
- ☐ :
- ☐ :

reflections:

Olusegun 'Sheg' Aranmolate

epoch one:
isochronal reflections (1)

epoch one:
isochronal reflections (2)

Olusegun 'Sheg' Aranmolate

day eleven:
the right attention

Love is the difficult realization that something other than oneself is real.
> Iris Murdoch (1919 - 1999)

At some point, you might have noticed that parents with toddlers usually have a tough time shopping in a store. It seems like every time these parents begin to look at store items their toddlers get fussy and upset because their parents aren't giving them undivided attention. Babies and toddlers, despite their sometimes extreme demands for affection, reveal two basic human features, which are our desire for attention and signs of approval from other people, and our disappointment when we don't get the needed attention.

I once heard the story of a professor at a prestigious university who had worked diligently for several years. Sadly, one day someone found him dead in his office. Apparently, his suicide note revealed that he killed himself because nobody cared about how he felt, only about how much he could contribute to the university. This story is sad because that institution lost a bright individual, at least in part, because it failed to show appreciation to its faculty. It is easy for us to get caught up in the webs of our society and fail to show our appreciation to people around us. Nevertheless, you might be surprised to find that a few kind words of appreciation and encouragement can do a lot of good. Take some time out of your busy life and compliment someone else. You never know—your kind words might be the difference between life and death.

schema:

body:
- ☐ eat a healthy breakfast.
- ☐ take multivitamins.
- ☐ eat lots of steamed vegetables.
- ☐ go for a jog.
- ☐ complete several standing rows.

mind:
- ☐ compliment others.
- ☐ inspire others.

goals:
- ☐ :
- ☐ :
- ☐ :

reflections:

day twelve:
exemplar

Reputation is what other people know about you. Honor is what you know about yourself.
Lois McMaster Bujold (1949 - ****)

You know what? A young, upcoming physicist is most likely mentored by a venerated physics professor. A young basketball player probably looks up to an older player for inspiration. A young actor usually mimics older well-established actors—the list keeps on going. The truth is that regardless of what path we decide to pursue in life, we tend to have role models that we look up to for advice and inspiration. Interestingly, overtime many of us become like our role models and tend to incorporate many of their fundamental values into our lives. Therefore, it is important for us to always look up to positive role models, not negative ones.

On several occasions, I have had several people ask me for my source of inspiration and the power that drives me to succeed in life. I tell them that although my passion for success comes from within, I get most of my inspiration from positive role models. Furthermore, I tell them that whenever I decide to try something new in life, I find people who have excelled greatly in doing it and strive to become as successful. Sometimes, I even imagine that these people are always judging my actions. Strangely, all this makes me act appropriately and work harder. Who do you look up to? Is it your parents, your teacher, your professor, a celebrity, or an athlete? Whoever it is, will this individual be impressed by your work ethics and the way you treat others? Or will they be disappointed? Think about the way your role models will react to your actions. Also remember that someone else might be looking up to you for inspiration, so always act appropriately towards others and be positive.

schema:

body:

- ☐ eat a healthy breakfast.
- ☐ take multivitamins.
- ☐ eat lots of fruits.
- ☐ complete several push-ups.
- ☐ complete several sit-ups.

mind:

- ☐ cherish today like it's your last.
- ☐ be compassionate to everyone.

goals:

- ☐ :
- ☐ :
- ☐ :

reflections:

Olusegun 'Sheg' Aranmolate

day thirteen:
talkative ones

Toil to make yourself remarkable by some talent or other.
Seneca (5 BC - 65 AD)

Nowadays, there is an unspoken rule about having a cell phone and it seems taboo not to have one. It's becoming really bad these days because many of us are becoming very condescending towards people who don't own cell phones. Crazily, more and more of us are becoming so attached to our phones that a day without it feels like being lost in the wilderness. It is also uncommon these days for a person to have a phone plan without unlimited nights and weekend minutes, and funny enough, many of us actually do use these minutes. In fact, if unlimited talk could be quantified, many of us will have talked unlimited times over the phone. Ridiculously, many of these conversations are about trivial issues.

It is good to call and talk to our family and friends, and to check on their wellbeing. However, when we start gossiping about others and spreading hateful thoughts and messages, then our phone talk becomes useless. Unfortunately, many of us have already spent what amounts to several days of our lives on the phone with nothing tangible to show for them, days we could have spent making a difference in our lives and in other people's lives. Have you ever taken the time to listen to your typical phone conversation? You might be surprised to find out that some of your conversations are empty and you could have better used the time you spent on those conversations. Surely, careless talk will bring you more trouble than peace. Thus, be careful of what you say, how you say it, and when you say it. Don't be like those annoying individuals on the bus or in the store, who talk loudly on their cell phones about nothing important, letting their valuable talents go to waste.

schema:

body:

- ☐ eat a healthy breakfast.
- ☐ take multivitamins.
- ☐ drink lots of white tea.
- ☐ take the stairs, instead of the elevator.
- ☐ complete several bench dips.

mind:

- ☐ be kind to everyone.
- ☐ talk less and listen more.

goals:

- ☐ :
- ☐ :
- ☐ :

reflections:

Olusegun 'Sheg' Aranmolate

day fourteen:
gratefulness

Gratitude is born in hearts that take time to count up past mercies.
> Charles E. Jefferson (1860 - 1937)

Once, I happened to be watching a television show about investor buying and selling homes for profit. It was exciting to see people "flipping" homes at fast rates and making sizable profits. These investors buy old homes, fix them up in a few weeks, and sell them for a profit. Yet, I noticed that many of these investors got upset whenever they sold a home lower than their initial asking price. The feeling of disappointment in these individuals is normal because they didn't get what they wanted. On the contrary, they failed to realize that things could have been much worse for them. For instance, they could have lost the home to a fire or a natural disaster, just to mention a few calamities.

The drive to become highly successful individuals is great to have, but sadly many of us get carried away with this desire that we become ungrateful and forgetful of all the good things around us. When we don't get the results that we want or when we get something less than what we bargained, it is important to always be thankful for our many blessings and to realize that life could be worse. Funny enough, many of us don't realize that the ability to complain about life is a luxury in itself. There are millions of people around the world who live in miserable conditions and don't have the luxury to complain about it. Take some time out of your busy life and drive to the nearby children's hospital. You will be saddened to see how much pain and suffering some little children endure everyday without complaining. Simply be thankful for the breath of life.

schema:

body:
- ☐ eat a healthy breakfast.
- ☐ take multivitamins.
- ☐ eat lots of seafood.
- ☐ complete several bicep curls.
- ☐ complete several lunges.

mind:
- ☐ be grateful.
- ☐ think positively.

goals:
- ☐ :
- ☐ :
- ☐ :

reflections:

day fifteen:
cool it

An unhurried sense of time is in itself a form of wealth.
Bonnie Friedman (1958 - ****)

What time is it? This is a typical question that you probably have been asked by someone else, and it is one of the few questions to which you and the several billion other people in the world can relate. We always want to know the time, because we have all of our activities invested in time. We pay our bills based on certain times of the month, we get paid according to how much time we spend working, and we celebrate special occasions based on certain times of the year. I was recently watching a movie and I heard an interesting statement about time, which suggested that time is simply a series of numbers with attached meanings, and without these meanings, time is nothing more than numbers. In all actuality, this description of time is correct. Time is a concept that was developed by humans, using numbers to keep track of events, and we indeed give these otherwise meaningless numbers power.

Many of us have become so engulfed by time that we literally have become slaves to it. Our every move and action is determined by the time, and many of us can't function without knowing the time. We have become so strung-out like addicts that we allow our fast paced and time-conscious lifestyles ruin our personal relationships. Of course, it will be ridiculous for anyone to completely ignore the time; however, everyday it is important for us to take some time off to breathe and recuperate. Use this period to think about and appreciate all those wonderful things around us, like our family, friends, pets, good food, scenic landscapes, and escape to a place where we can relax and forget about all the worries we have attached to time.

schema:

body:
- ☐ eat a healthy breakfast.
- ☐ take multivitamins.
- ☐ eat lots of fresh salad.
- ☐ stretch several times.
- ☐ clean your home.

mind:
- ☐ meditate.
- ☐ prioritize your life.

goals:
- ☐ :
- ☐ :
- ☐ :

reflections:

day sixteen:
rage

When anger rises, think of the consequences.
Confucius (551 BC - 479 BC)

I was watching the television one morning, and happened to catch a news exclusive that focused on the aftermath of a tornado storm on a small town. The tornado had literally destroyed the entire town and its important landmarks. The schools, libraries, shops and all other important buildings were all shattered to pieces, and I remember watching several of the town members cry and lament on how quick the tornado had destroyed their homes. These people's lamentations, in a unique way, got me thinking about anger and its damaging effects.

The repercussion of our anger can very much be like a wild tornado, rapidly advancing through a town, producing tremendous irreversible damage along the way. There are so many of us who have seriously hurt ourselves and our loved one because we let our anger take control of our actions. Our anger burst usually begins with someone or something ticking us off and suddenly we unleash our severely damaging "inner tornado." Do you remember the last time you got angry? Did you say or do things that you normally will not say or do? Did you hurt people that you wouldn't normally hurt? Anger is a powerful emotion that can destroy and has destroyed many great people. Remember that just as nature controls the occurrence of tornadoes, we have the ability to control our actions based on anger. Hence, next time someone angers you, before you let go, take a moment to think about all the damage that could result if you let your anger take the best of you.

schema:

body:
- ☐ eat a healthy breakfast.
- ☐ take multivitamins.
- ☐ drink lots of fresh juice.
- ☐ complete several sit-ups.
- ☐ complete several shoulder presses.

mind:
- ☐ take a mental vacation.
- ☐ smile and greet everyone.

goals:
- ☐ :
- ☐ :
- ☐ :

reflections:

Olusegun 'Sheg' Aranmolate

day seventeen:
my deadline

Nothing is stronger than habit.
    Ovid (43 BC - 17 AD)

Deadlines! Everyday of our lives, we are confronted with one deadline or another. Nowadays, it seems like every aspect of our lives has a deadline, from our tasks at work, to our bills at home, to our assignments at school, everything has a deadline. We all know from experience that failure to meet these deadlines usually results in some type of penalty. Interestingly, the fear of being penalized is the driving force that motivates many of us to complete our tasks. In fact, so many of us have become so accustomed to deadlines that we can't function optimally without some sort of deadline. Let's assume that your boss at work gave you two days to complete an important task that affected the entire structure of your company. Obviously, if you wanted to keep your job, you will work really hard to complete the task in the allotted time.

It's ironic that many of us strive to complete deadlines set by others but fail to complete deadlines set by ourselves. I have worked with several people, who frequently set personal deadlines for themselves, such as living a healthy lifestyle, joining a gym, or even ditching a bad habit. However, these individuals never accomplished their goals. Honestly, many of us fail to meet our deadlines because we don't get penalized upon failure. To get around this problem, we need to become more accountable for our actions and penalize ourselves whenever we fail to meet our deadlines. You will be amazed that this mentality will motivate and help you accomplish your set goals. Quit failing and letting yourself down! Take better care of your life and remember that your personal deadlines are just as important as any other deadline.

schema:

body:

- ☐ eat a healthy breakfast.
- ☐ take multivitamins.
- ☐ eat some chocolate.
- ☐ complete several push-ups.
- ☐ complete several lunges.

mind:

- ☐ laugh at every chance.
- ☐ apologize for your faults.

goals:

- ☐ :
- ☐ :
- ☐ :

reflections:

day eighteen:
more junk

Junk is the ultimate merchandise. The junk merchant does not sell his product to the consumer, he sells the consumer to the product. He does not improve and simplify his merchandise, he degrades and simplifies the client.
William S. Burroughs (1914 - 1997)

Whenever, I walk into a thrift store, I always get amazed by the large amounts of "stuff" that are up for sale and by the fluctuation between the ratio of items that I consider to be valuable and those that I consider to be valueless. These observations clearly confirm that there is a constant interchange between donated and purchased items. It also strengthens the age-old adage that one person's trash is another person's treasure. Unquestionably, humans have a constant thirst for "stuff," especially material stuff, and we are always out to replace or replenish our old "stuff" with more "stuff," either old or new.

There's no doubt that we live in a material world, and unfortunately many of us have become so engulfed by all the materialism that we tend to forget the important aspects of life that really matter, such as our family, our friends, and good relationships with people. Have you ever had the chance to visit an estate auction? If so, then you know that all the material things we acquire during our lifetime will do us no good at the time of our demise. I don't, in anyway, imply or want to imply that we should suffer and experience life without material pleasures. However, we should be more in-tune with ourselves and more conscious of the people around us, so that we don't miss out on the truly beautiful aspects of life. Remember that true friendship is more important and valuable than any riches in the world. Riches vanish with time, but true friendship strengthens with each passing day.

schema:

body:
- ☐ eat a healthy breakfast.
- ☐ take multivitamins.
- ☐ drink lots of green tea.
- ☐ go for a jog.
- ☐ complete several squats.

mind:
- ☐ meditate.
- ☐ be compassionate to everyone.

goals:
- ☐ :
- ☐ :
- ☐ :

reflections:

day nineteen:
always be primed

In preparing for battle I have always found that plans are useless, but planning is indispensable.
Dwight D. Eisenhower (1890 - 1969)

Sometimes, when I am done shopping in the mall and happen to have some idle time, I head towards the food court to eat and relax my aching feet. During these times, I watch the actions and behaviors of several people in the mall. There are the window-shoppers who gaze randomly in awe, the causal-shoppers who are easily distracted by sale items, and the resolute-shoppers who always seem to be rushed. Interestingly, I have noticed that all these different types of shoppers, despite all occupying the same confined mall space seem to be driven by the same thing: impulsivity. Though, some are more blatant than others, the fact remains that the choices and actions of these people are impulsively driven by the lights, the sales, and several other attractive features of the mall.

No doubt, we can be sporadic and spontaneous in our choices and actions. This characteristic can be good, such as when it comes to artistic creativity. However, it can also be a deterrent, like when we need to make important life decisions. Once, I talked to a young woman, who had recently graduated from college. Unlike most graduates who are elated about graduation, she was frustrated because she felt she had chosen her major on impulse and graduated with a degree that she disliked. Regrettably, many of us are like this woman because we become sad after making impulsive choices that become grave mistakes. Regardless of any impulsive choice you have made, realize that what's done is done and that you can't let your mistakes take you prisoner. Learn from those mistakes, move-on with your life, and always make plans for your next big decisions. All this will help you to avoid making impulsive decisions.

schema:

body:
- ☐ eat a healthy breakfast.
- ☐ take multivitamins.
- ☐ eat lots of fruits.
- ☐ complete several bench dips.
- ☐ play with friends and family.

mind:
- ☐ inspire others.
- ☐ be proactive.

goals:
- ☐ :
- ☐ :
- ☐ :

reflections:

day twenty:
<u>our legacy</u>

With regard to excellence, it is not enough to know, but we must try to have and use it.
Aristotle (384 BC - 322 BC)

When a person retires, they are usually honored with some sort of acknowledgment ceremony and the retiree becomes replaced by a successor. However, the story of a once-brilliant professor whose retirement didn't fit the norm got me thinking about the importance of our legacy. Apparently, this professor was once a respected scholar, whose scientific contributions to academia were invaluable. However, as years passed, he began to abuse alcohol, which severely interfered with his social and intellectual abilities. Interestingly, despite his alcohol abuse, he wasn't fired because he was under an academic tenure contract. Nevertheless, a couple more years of boozing led the university to force him into an "early retirement." Regrettably, as soon as he retired the university closed his office and never filled his position, because he had already been replaced long before he left.

It is unfortunate that intelligent individuals sometimes make grave mistakes and embark on the path towards self-destruction. Also, it's a pity that because we live in a somewhat cruel world, people remember some of us (like this professor) for our failures, not all our great successes. Therefore, it is important that we avoid placing ourselves in compromising positions that tarnish our reputation and focus on our given tasks so that when we do vacate our jobs, our presence will be missed and a replacement will be desperately needed. Don't be the reason why everyone around you is stagnant. Always give your best so that at the end, you have an honorable legacy for your successors to follow. Furthermore, always show compassion to those people who are in pain and sadly seek outlets that often end in tragedy. If you are a troubled individual, please seek immediate help.

schema:

body:
- ☐ eat a healthy breakfast.
- ☐ take multivitamins.
- ☐ drink lots of water.
- ☐ stretch several times.
- ☐ get a massage.

mind:
- ☐ think positively.
- ☐ take a mental vacation.

goals:
- ☐ :
- ☐ :
- ☐ :

reflections:

epoch two:
<u>isochronal reflections (1)</u>

epoch two:
<u>isochronal reflections (2)</u>

day twenty - one:
<u>the philanthropist</u>

The excellence of a gift lies in its appropriateness rather than in its value.
Charles Dudley Warner (1829 - 1900)

Once, I was at a meeting and before it started, we were all asked to introduce ourselves. One by one, each person began by stating their name, their age and their profession. When it came my turn to speak, I introduced myself and said that I was a philanthropist by profession. As expected, at this announcement, I heard people in the room chuckle, and one guy in the group said, "Come on, you're not a philanthropist, what do you really do for a living?" The guy's question was sincere, but unfortunate because like several other people, he still had a rudimentary idea of a philanthropist, which was probably a wealthy older individual who for altruistic reasons donates money to charity. Ironically, there are several wealthy individuals who regularly donate to charity, solely for opportunistic reasons.

A philanthropist is anyone who constantly strives to benefit and better humanity, and you don't have to be a millionaire or billionaire, you simply need to possess a genuine desire to help others. Interestingly, the concept of philanthropy is relative to the recipient. For instance, a starving homeless man will consider you a bigger philanthropist than the everyday person, if you gave him a hot delicious meal. Honestly, philanthropy doesn't have anything to do with how much money you have in the bank, rather how much affection you have in your heart. Don't be one of those people who reinforce the philanthropist stereotype, rather be a good example and show others that you don't have to be extremely rich to make a difference in another person's life. Become a philanthropist today and make your world, no matter how small or large, a better place for others to inhabit.

schema:

body:
- ☐ eat a healthy breakfast.
- ☐ take multivitamins.
- ☐ eat lots of fish.
- ☐ go for a jog.
- ☐ complete several push-ups.

mind:
- ☐ inspire others.
- ☐ breathe and introspect.

goals:
- ☐ :
- ☐ :
- ☐ :

reflections:

Olusegun 'Sheg' Aranmolate

day twenty - two:
<u>walking away</u>

Strong reasons make strong actions.
William Shakespeare (1564 - 1616)

Sometimes, many of us don't realize or seem to forget that a lot of our actions, both good and bad, are directly influenced by our external environment. For example, if you walked into a restaurant and the host at the door immediately gave you a nasty attitude, it is likely that you will immediately be ticked-off and you will respond rudely as well. Likewise, if the host's initial response was polite and friendly, except you were already upset or having a crappy day, you will respond politely as well.

The truth is that we often allow other people to define our actions and determine the way we feel. Funny enough, we, humans, pride ourselves on our possession and ability to exercise freewill, but we often don't utilize this innate ability and let other people dictate the way we feel. Take a moment to think about the last time you became upset or angry. Was it solely your own doing or was it the result of someone else imposing their actions and emotions on you? Honestly, there is no reason why we should put ourselves in a position that allows others to determine the way we feel or act. We can be a lot more peaceful with ourselves and with the people around us, if we consciously take control of our emotions and avoid mimicking other people's negative actions. Thus, next time someone talks or acts rudely towards you, instead of getting all fired up, respond politely and walk away. At the end of the day, you will be astonished by the peaceful outcomes of your freewill to transform a negative situation.

schema:

body:

- ☐ eat a healthy breakfast.
- ☐ take multivitamins.
- ☐ eat lots of fruits.
- ☐ take the stairs, instead of the elevator.
- ☐ complete several lunges.

mind:

- ☐ control your emotions.
- ☐ compliment others.

goals:

- ☐ :
- ☐ :
- ☐ :

reflections:

day twenty - three:
<u>paranoid</u>

Guilt is anger directed at ourselves—at what we did or did not do.
Peter McWilliams (1949 - 2000)

Remember when you were a child and your parents told you not to touch or play with a particular household item because it was fragile or expensive. Nevertheless, as soon as your parents weren't around, you disobeyed and played with it, only to end up breaking it like they had predicted. Then, immediately afterwards, you become scared of being caught and frantically try to hide the damage. Suddenly, every time your parents are nearby, your heart begins to pound out of fear of being "busted." This sudden behavioral change is simply the effects of our guilt taking a psychological toll on us. Interestingly, this situation occurs in adults as well. However, unlike children who are usually guilty of issues that involve disobedience, adults are usually guilty of issues that involve trust.

The typical adult guilt trip begins when we say or do hurtful things to others behind their backs and because of our guilt, we become angry, defensive, and even paranoid. We automatically assume that everyone will act similarly to ourselves and we feel that everyone knows our dirty secrets. Relax! It's impossible for everyone to know all those hurtful things we might have done to others and not everyone is going to act like we did. Guilt is a powerful emotion that can make the sanest of people insane. The next time you are feeling guilty for your actions, don't let it consume you, instead tell the truth to the person you hurt. You might be surprised that the consequences of telling the truth are far less tormenting than your guilt. Don't become consumed by the paranoia of your guilt, just let it all out and be free!

schema:

body:

- ☐ eat a healthy breakfast.
- ☐ take multivitamins.
- ☐ eat lots of stem vegetables.
- ☐ complete several sit-ups.
- ☐ go for a walk.

mind:

- ☐ apologize for your faults.
- ☐ appreciate nature

goals:

- ☐ :
- ☐ :
- ☐ :

reflections:

Olusegun 'Sheg' Aranmolate

day twenty - four:
different seasons

In these matters the only certainty is that nothing is certain.
Pliny the Elder (23 AD - 79 AD)

It should come as no surprise to anyone that the weather has different seasons. Where I live, summer is characterized by high daily temperatures and bright sunshine. Autumn has high winds and falling leaves. Winter is usually filled with snow and low temperatures, while spring brings beautiful flowers and green grasses. We realize that, no matter where we live, seasonal changes are natural occurrences, and consequently we don't get bothered by these changes. In fact, many of us will become worried and anxious, if this normal cycle was, in anyway, interrupted.

Our lives are seasonal like the weather. As a result, there are times when life is relatively easy and times when it becomes tough. However, because many of us usually fail to realize the impermanent nature of our problems, we usually become elated during good times and saddened when the rough gets going. Interestingly, every season in nature can be comfortable or uncomfortable, depending on how well one is dressed. For example, if you wore warm clothes during the summer and light clothes during the winter, you will be uncomfortable in both weather conditions because you're wearing the wrong clothing. Similarly in life, we need to dress appropriately with the correct "emotional clothes" to tackle the different seasons in our lives. Are you going through tough times in your life and does it seem never-ending? These moments, like the weather, are temporary and will soon be over. Always ensure that you have the right mindset and correct gear when you tackle the rough seasons of life, while, of course, enjoying the good seasons.

schema:

body:
- ☐ eat a healthy breakfast.
- ☐ take multivitamins.
- ☐ eat lots of steamed vegetables.
- ☐ complete several push-ups.
- ☐ complete several squats.

mind:
- ☐ think positively.
- ☐ be kind to everyone.

goals:
- ☐ :
- ☐ :
- ☐ :

reflections:

day twenty - five:
<u>grumbler</u>

Practice means to perform, over and over again in the face of all obstacles, some act of vision, of faith, of desire. Practice is a means of inviting the perfection desired.
Martha Graham (1894-1991)

It is normal for us to sometimes feel unaccomplished, especially when we compare our lives to highly successful people in the world who have achieved so much in their lifetime. Without trivializing our own accomplishments, we must realize that these feelings can trigger us to pursue greater success. Though, constantly worrying about our relatively little achievements can eventually become a serious problem. Fortunately, I have had the opportunity to speak with several successful people and I have noticed that these people always have a positive outlook on life, never worry excessively, and have an inextinguishable drive to succeed through good and bad times.

I honestly get disheartened when I hear people complain that their inability to succeed in life is primarily due to such things as their gender, race, or background. Every one of us has the ability to become successful in some sense, but many of us become stalled in life because of excuses. Take ants, for example. Compared to humans, ants are small, weak, and dumb. Nevertheless, these insects never quit doing their duties, like gathering food or building parts of their ant colony. Each ant, in doing so, becomes successful in helping fellow ants. In the future, whenever you are feeling worthless or intimidated by a daunting task, take a moment to think about busy ants in the woods and how much they accomplish daily. As I mentioned, we are much bigger and smarter than ants, so we really have few legitimate excuses for not pursuing success. We must quit complaining and start completing our given tasks.

schema:

body:

- ☐ eat a healthy breakfast.
- ☐ take multivitamins.
- ☐ drink lots of green tea.
- ☐ take the stairs, instead of the elevator.
- ☐ complete several push-ups.

mind:

- ☐ talk less and listen more.
- ☐ appreciate yourself.

goals:

- ☐ :
- ☐ :
- ☐ :

reflections:

day twenty - six:
<u>over the limit</u>

Never exceed your rights, and they will soon become unlimited.
  Jean Jacques Rousseau (1712 - 1778)

Whenever we walk into an elevator, the first thing we usually do is look at the left or right-hand side for the elevator buttons. However, there are several other features in the elevator that many of us don't always seem to notice, such as the fire warning signs and the elevator weight limit. The law requires every elevator to place a legible sign that shows the weight limit and the maximum number of people that can be carried at a particular instance. You don't need to have an advanced physics degree to realize that it will be dangerous to operate any elevator once the maximum weight limit is exceeded because the consequences can be disastrous.

Funny enough, in a strange way, our temperament is like an elevator with set weight limits. Obviously, different elevators have different weight capacities and as a result some elevators can carry more people than others. Likewise, some of us can handle larger emotional loads than others. Nonetheless, we all still have our limits and just like in the elevators, these limits are often ignored or unnoticed by others. Sadly, due to our nonchalant attitude, we often push and push others, especially our loved ones, until they snap and collapse like an unstable bridge. Be compassionate and pay more attention to other people's emotional threshold. Don't continue to push others over their emotional limits, just like you will not want others to push you over your limit.

schema:

body:
- ☐ eat a healthy breakfast.
- ☐ take multivitamins.
- ☐ drink lots of water.
- ☐ go for a jog.
- ☐ complete several sit-ups.

mind:
- ☐ practice tolerance.
- ☐ breathe and introspect.

goals:
- ☐ :
- ☐ :
- ☐ :

reflections:

Olusegun 'Sheg' Aranmolate

day twenty - seven:
speak out

The people who are the most bigoted are the people who have no convictions at all.
G. K. Chesterton (1874 - 1936)

Suppose you were taking a walk around your neighborhood and suddenly, as you passed a tree, you heard the sound of a child in distress. Immediately, you look behind the trees, and to your surprise you find an older child torturing an adorable toddler. Any adult in their right mind will be stunned by the older child's actions and would immediately stop the child from inflicting anymore pain to the toddler. Some might even go further as to taking the toddler away from the older child and reporting the incident to the parents of both children, if they happen to know them.

This response to such a situation is due to our sense of justice, which is aroused by the sight of injustice and gives us an incentive to correct such unfairness. However, many of us fail to utilize this authority, when it comes to situations that directly affect our comfort and happiness. Why do many of us continuously allow others to take advantage of our weaknesses and mistreat us on a daily basis, without ever voicing our opinions? There are times in our lives when we will be mistreated like the toddler, but unfortunately there may not be anyone but ourselves to defend us. Therefore, it is important for us to learn how to stand up against such tyranny and abuse. Today, not tomorrow, is your day of liberation from those bad habits as well as demeaning and oppressive individuals who consciously or subconsciously try to humiliate you. Peacefully stand up against the oppression and let your voice be heard!

schema:

body:

- ☐ eat a healthy breakfast.
- ☐ take multivitamins.
- ☐ eat some chocolate.
- ☐ stretch several times.
- ☐ go for a walk.

mind:

- ☐ relax to music.
- ☐ laugh at every chance.

goals:

- ☐ :
- ☐ :
- ☐ :

reflections:

day twenty - eight:
intricate connection

The greatest friend of Truth is time, her greatest enemy is Prejudice, and her constant companion Humility.
Charles Caleb Colton (1780 - 1832)

If you have ever watched a documentary that depicts wild beasts like Lions, Tigers, and Antelopes in their natural habitat, then you realize that these animals on a daily basis are constantly battling the harsh elements in nature. These documentaries reveal that there are complex interactions between different animals, especially when it comes to feeding. This complex interaction in biology is called the food web, where all animals on earth are directly or indirectly connected to each other by their desire to feed. Accordingly, the ferocious meat-eating Lion is ultimately dependent on grass because the Lion eats many animals that depend on grass for survival. As a result, without grass, the herbivorous animals that the Lions eat will all die from starvation and without these animals the Lions will also be on their way to extinction.

Humans, similarly, coexist in a world with intricate connections, whereby the input of several people from different walks of life is required for the proper functioning of our society. Sadly, many of us get carried away by our societal status and forget how we are all dependent on each other. For example, the auto-mechanic needs the doctor on sick days, the doctor needs the mechanic to fix his or her car, and the doctor needs the janitor to have clean hospitals. Even more so, think about those nasty drivers who cut you off in traffic. You might not immediately realize it, but you are indeed dependent on those persons to pay their taxes. Don't be obnoxious with your social status and make a conscious decision today to start treating everyone with respect. Remember that in a mysterious way we are all dependent on each other, just as Lions are dependent on grass.

schema:

body:

- ☐ eat a healthy breakfast.
- ☐ take multivitamins.
- ☐ eat lots of yogurt.
- ☐ complete several bench dips.
- ☐ play with friends and family.

mind:

- ☐ practice tolerance.
- ☐ think positively.

goals:

- ☐ :
- ☐ :
- ☐ :

reflections:

Olusegun 'Sheg' Aranmolate

day twenty - nine:
<u>harsh words</u>

For me, words are a form of action, capable of influencing change.
Ingrid Bengis (1944 - ****)

During my sophomore year in college, I decided that I wanted to obtain a second degree in psychology, and to do so I needed to take several psychology courses, one of which was abnormal psychology. In this class, I got to watch several educative videos, and learn a lot about the fragility and vulnerability of the human mind. I remember watching a touching documentary about a group of women who were living with or recovering from severe eating disorders. Sadly, many of these beautiful women said that their disorders began when someone, usually a loved one, had verbally abused them or had called them fat. For me, this confirmed that our words are powerful enough to physically and psychologically hurt others.

Many of us are often oblivious of the power and irreparable damage that our words can inflict on others. Simply put, our mouths can be like loaded guns with bullets made of words, and just as unlocked guns can misfire if incorrectly handled, careless mouths can also misfire. For this reason, we have to be careful of what we say and how and when we say it because our words could misfire and severely hurt our loved ones. In the future, when you are "pissed-off" and want to say hurtful words to someone else, take a moment to think about the possible psychological effects that could result from those words. Remember that once those words are out of your mouth, they have become part of history and can never be retrieved or taken back. Be careful! You never know your words might be the difference between a happy and a broken person.

schema:

body:

- ☐ eat a healthy breakfast.
- ☐ take multivitamins.
- ☐ eat some of chocolate.
- ☐ complete several sit-ups.
- ☐ complete several lunges.

mind:

- ☐ visualize a successful day.
- ☐ breathe and introspect.

goals:

- ☐ :
- ☐ :
- ☐ :

reflections:

day thirty:
<u>fight it</u>

Choose the life that is most useful, and habit will make it the most agreeable.
Sir Francis Bacon (1561 - 1626)

Toddlers are adorable and curious little beings, and many of them, at the slightest opportunity, place any object, edible or poisonous, into their mouths for munching. If you ask any parent, they will tell you that they're always looking for dangerous objects that their child might try swallowing. Thus, any reasonable parent should know that it is unwise to leave an opened bottle of prescription pills close to a toddler because it is very likely that the child will consume the pills. Fascinatingly, many of us, as adults, although we will not want to compare ourselves to toddlers, act and behave like toddlers, especially when it comes to managing our addictions.

It's obvious that different people have different addictions, some of which are socially acceptable and others socially repulsive. Nevertheless, if your addiction is harmful to your health and is ruining your relationship with your loved ones, then you have to ditch that habit—keep yourself away from it! Many of us, like toddlers, are unable to control ourselves in the presence of our addictive substances. For example, people trying to quit smoking, find it hard to resist cigarettes, when amongst people who are smoking. Our difficulty in resisting temptations isn't because we're losers, rather because of our flawed biological makeup. However, we need to become more responsible (like parents of toddlers), and continually remove harmful and addictive substances from our vicinity. For instance, if you're trying to quit smoking or junk food, never buy or stock your homes with these things. Keeping your eyes and mind away from addictive substances can help you prevent a relapse. When it comes to our addictions, always remember that "out of sight is out of mind."

schema:

body:
- ☐ eat a healthy breakfast.
- ☐ take multivitamins.
- ☐ eat lots of fruits.
- ☐ complete several shoulder presses.
- ☐ complete several calf-raises.

mind:
- ☐ meditate.
- ☐ take a mental vacation.

goals:
- ☐ :
- ☐ :
- ☐ :

reflections:

epoch three:
<u>isochronal reflections (1)</u>

epoch three:
isochronal reflections (2)

day thirty - one:
<u>finding happy</u>

The pursuit of happiness is a most ridiculous phrase; if you pursue happiness you'll never find it.
C. P. Snow (1905 - 1980)

I was once window-shopping in an upscale jewelry store that sold expensive stones. While I was glancing at the jewelries, I noticed two women in the store. The first woman wasn't wearing jewelry and was neatly dressed in casual clothes, while the other woman, in stark contrast, wore a huge, expensive looking necklace and designer clothes. As I continued window-shopping, I immediately concluded that the woman in the expensive clothes was rich and the other woman in the causal clothes was simply window-shopping, like myself. Surprisingly, it turned out that the woman in the casual clothes was the owner of the store, inspecting her merchandise; the woman in the designer clothes was the window-shopper!

Many at times, we make assumptions solely based on what we see. For instance, we see a person nicely dressed and immediately assume that they are financially successful and happy. The truth, however, is that looks can be deceiving, and all that glitters is not platinum. Over the years, I have come to realize that many wealthy people who are happy with life have relatively normal lives and average lifestyles. This is because they know that extravagance or excessive spending doesn't bring happiness. Don't be fooled by a person's outward appearance alone because there are lots of financially successful people who are emotionally destitute, begging for the slightest signs of happiness. Save yourself the heartache and realize that if you're never happy with less, you can't be happy with more.

schema:

body:
- ☐ eat a healthy breakfast.
- ☐ take multivitamins.
- ☐ eat lots of steamed vegetables.
- ☐ complete several bench dips.
- ☐ go for a walk.

mind:
- ☐ appreciate yourself.
- ☐ think positively.

goals:
- ☐ :
- ☐ :
- ☐ :

reflections:

day thirty - two:
<u>rock bottom</u>

Nothing fails like success.
 Gerald Nachman (1938 - ****)

There are times in our lives when we become unhappy, feeling like our lives have reached rock-bottom. Such miserable times are often the effects of drastic changes in our lives, such as the loss of or estrangement from a loved one, health problems, financial difficulties, or sometimes no apparent reason. Regardless of the cause or reason, the truth is that these moments make us feel worthless like our entire world has hopelessly crashed down. If we took a closer look at our situation, however, we will usually realize that we can use the rock-bottom feeling as an incentive to improve and turn around our lives.

Rock-bottom is the lowest possible point that we could find ourselves and because our lives can't get any worse, it can be a unique opportunity for us to reevaluate the composition of our foundation and rebuild our lives for the better. For example, if a rock-climber rapidly ascends up a mountain, but due to inexperience of the terrain, grabs onto a loose rock and falls to the bottom (literally rock-bottom!), then, during the next climb, this climber will know how to avoid such a pratfall that send people crashing down. Do you feel full of despair or like you've reached rock-bottom? Remember that rock-bottom can be a grand opportunity to start afresh and set things right. Don't let your sorrows take the best of you. Instead, garner all your strength and all your previously acquired knowledge and climb higher than ever before!

schema:

body:
- ☐ eat a healthy breakfast.
- ☐ take multivitamins.
- ☐ drink lots of water.
- ☐ go for a jog.
- ☐ complete several squats.

mind:
- ☐ be kind to everyone.
- ☐ inspire others.

goals:
- ☐ :
- ☐ :
- ☐ :

reflections:

Olusegun 'Sheg' Aranmolate

day thirty - three:
<u>fashion style</u>

People grow through experience if they meet life honestly and courageously. This is how character is built.
Eleanor Roosevelt (1884 - 1962)

When we wake up each morning, we usually have a daily routine, including, among other things, brushing our teeth, taking a shower, and drinking coffee. Still, there comes a point when we have to decide what clothes to wear and usually turn to the weather forecast for guidance. Of course, we primarily wear clothes to cover our nakedness and to protect us from the elements of nature, such as the heat, the cold, and insects. But also, we wear clothes for special occasions and to show off social status or one's sense of style. Sadly enough, many of us have become engulfed and enslaved by the showing off aspect of clothes.

We have become so concerned with our clothes that we allow our feelings to be governed by what we wear. For instance, I have met several people who become unhappy if they feel their clothes aren't fashionable. Honestly, we need to stop worrying excessively about our clothes because they fade and rip with time. Rather, we should start focusing on our "emotional clothes," i.e. the positive emotions we show other people. If there was a way to judge people by their emotional clothes, it may come as no surprise that some of us are poorly dressed in rags of anger, despair, and even hatred. Clean out your emotional closet of those clothes and replace them with clothes of kindness, compassion, and honesty. People will definitely appreciate and even desire your new emotional style.

schema:

body:
- ☐ eat a healthy breakfast.
- ☐ take multivitamins.
- ☐ drink lots of white tea.
- ☐ stretch several times.
- ☐ complete several push-ups.

mind:
- ☐ relax with music.
- ☐ breathe and introspect.

goals:
- ☐ :
- ☐ :
- ☐ :

reflections:

day thirty - four:
dynamic change

Never confuse movement with action.
Ernest Hemingway (1899 - 1961)

Suppose that one day, while you are watching your favorite TV show, a commercial for a charitable organization begins, pleading for funds to feed a bunch of starving children with large oversized bellies. These types of commercials usually make us sad because we are generally kind-hearted by nature and hate to see others suffer. After the commercial, many of us will probably complain about all the injustice and greed in the world, and further conclude that those starving kids will be better off if more rich people gave to the poor. The truth, however, is that many of us, in our rants against the rich, fail to identify our own greed and inadequacy.

Wealth is relative. For instance, a millionaire is poorer than a billionaire, but to a person with only a few pennies, both people are extremely rich. Honestly, many of us have enough money and resources to give to the needy, but because of our numerous excuses usually end up doing nothing. We're like broken cell phones that are capable of receiving incoming calls but incapable of making outgoing calls. Everyday, we receive so much information on the suffering of others, yet we do absolutely nothing to change the world. Ironically, these disheartening issues sometimes become the latest gossip amongst those people who actually care about the news. Change in our society requires consciously taking action, and every one of us has the ability to produce positive change. Next time don't just complain about other people's inaction and those issues that affect your families, friends, and humanity, do something to help out. Remember that actions always speak louder than words, and words always speak louder than absolute silence.

schema:

body:

- ☐ eat a healthy breakfast.
- ☐ take multivitamins.
- ☐ eat lots of fresh salad.
- ☐ complete several push-ups.
- ☐ get a massage.

mind:

- ☐ inspire others to change.
- ☐ prioritize your day.

goals:

- ☐ :
- ☐ :
- ☐ :

reflections:

day thirty - five:
<u>steady moves</u>

You can't wait for inspiration. You have to go after it with a club.
> Jack London (1876 - 1916)

I once tutored children in elementary school. On my first day with the kids, in order to gauge their perception of the world, I always ask them what they wanted to do as adults. Many of the kids had great choices, such as lawyers, doctors, teachers, and police officers. I was amazed that kids are so conscious of the world around them and harbor great desires to make it better. Unfortunately, as they become older and are subjected to harsh realities in the world, some of their amazing plans never get executed or accomplished. The same occurs with the dreams of some adults, like ending world starvation and curing human diseases.

Many of us never get to fulfill our dreams not because we are procrastinators—actually maybe we are slight procrastinators! The truth, however, is that we live in a world filled with responsibilities. We are consumed with caring for our families and paying our bills that we consequently have little time to execute many of our great ideas. Nevertheless, our responsibilities shouldn't be a reason for us to forgo all our dreams, rather an incentive for us to complete them. You can't build your dream home overnight, just as you can't change the entire world in one night. However, by taking a few minutes out of each day you can pursue parts of your dreams. If you're genuinely keen on making a difference in the world, you should start by improving yourself, then your family, your community, and finally the entire world. Remember that the great pyramids of Giza were built block by block.

schema:

body:
- ☐ eat a healthy breakfast.
- ☐ take multivitamins.
- ☐ drink lots of green tea.
- ☐ go for a jog.
- ☐ complete several bicep curls.

mind:
- ☐ be more proactive.
- ☐ cherish today like it's your last.

goals:
- ☐ :
- ☐ :
- ☐ :

reflections:

day thirty - six:
<u>reconstruction</u>

A good name, like good will, is got by many actions and lost
by one.
  Lord Jeffery (1773 - 1850)

Recently, I visited my old college to see old friends and
professors, and was amazed by how much the campus, in only
a few years, had changed. Constructors erected several new
buildings and there were other construction projects in progress.
I noticed that the students and many new professors looked
much younger than when I was there. I suddenly came to the
sad realization that I was getting older and my beloved college
had changed without me. Change, after all, is a part of life and
we are always changing our environment through continual
planned demolition and construction projects. For instance, we
demolish old bridges so we can construct, stronger, better
bridges. Old buildings are converted to sky scrappers, and the
list continues.

Our lives can be similar to a construction project. Sometimes
we learn new facts and experience new situations that require
us to demolish and reconstruct our views and perspectives of
the world. Often, these newly-formed ideas are stronger than
the older ones. If you are familiar with construction, then you
know it can take several years to build a large building like a
skyscraper or cathedral, but only a few seconds to destroy it.
Similarly, many of us also take years to construct our
architecturally sound lives, but sadly demolish them with one
simple mistake. Remember that we live in a world that requires
change and no matter how wonderful your life may seem one
slipup can cost you everything. Always be patient in forming
your ideas, don't be afraid to reconstruct them if you are wrong,
and avoid those destructive elements that can ruin your life.
Nevertheless, with time and patience, you can always rebuild
your life, no matter how bad you may have "ruined" it.

schema:

body:

- ☐ eat a healthy breakfast.
- ☐ take multivitamins.
- ☐ eat some chocolate.
- ☐ play with friends and family.
- ☐ complete several sit-ups.

mind:

- ☐ practice tolerance.
- ☐ smile and greet everyone.

goals:

- ☐ :
- ☐ :
- ☐ :

reflections:

Olusegun 'Sheg' Aranmolate

day thirty - seven:
<u>active gestures</u>

Never doubt that a small group of thoughtful, committed citizens can change the world. Indeed, it is the only thing that ever has.
> Margaret Mead (1901 - 1978)

If you have ever walked on the busy streets of one of the many developing nations, then surely you encountered malnourished children, begging desperately for food or some money. Sadly, because of the multitude of these children on the streets, many of their cries and pleas are often shunned by stoic adults. Nevertheless, some adults are still touched by their plight and will stop to offer them food or money. Unfortunately, overtime many of these initially compassionate adults also become callous to the suffering of these children, not because they are terrible people, rather because they join the masses and accept defeat, concluding that the suffering of these children is a normal part of their society.

All humans, by default and by the characterization as being "human," are equal, and there shouldn't be any reason, why one person should enjoy and another should suffer things like starvation and terrible living conditions. How will you like to be one of those orphans starving daily, only to hear adults conclude that your pain is a normal part of society? It's undeniable that we live in a world filled with much pain and suffering. Many of us, however, are fortunate enough and have the ability to make a positive difference in our unjust world. Remember that the entire world is our home, and just as we can't leave all the chores and maintenance to one parent or sibling, we can't leave the eradication of the world's problems to one nation or person. Instead, we should all take active roles in our communities and society to ensure that we minimize the suffering of other people.

---

schema:

body:
- ☐ eat a healthy breakfast.
- ☐ take multivitamins.
- ☐ eat lots of yogurt.
- ☐ complete several bicep curls.
- ☐ complete several bench dips.

mind:
- ☐ think positively.
- ☐ meditate.

goals:
- ☐ :
- ☐ :
- ☐ :

reflections:

day thirty - eight:
<u>blissful manners</u>

The greatest griefs are those we cause ourselves.
  Sophocles (496 BC - 406 BC)

Happiness and sadness are two common emotions, and beginning in childhood, society teaches us that it is good to be happy and bad to be sad. Surely, we become happy when we hear good news and saddened when we hear bad news. As a result, we are all quite familiar with the tingling feel-good sensation of happiness and the overall burning sensation of sadness. Interestingly, despite these disparate sensations of happiness and sadness, many of us, in a matter of seconds, can quickly switch from being happy to being sad, but can't quickly switch from being sad to being happy. Literally, one minute we're happy and the next minute we feel like we've never experienced happiness in our lives.

Why don't we feel sad, when we hear good news and happy when we hear bad news? In theory, it's possible because our "defined" emotions, such as happiness, sadness, or anger are the combination of certain feelings attached to words. Thus, technically, the feeling of happiness in one person can be very different in another person. For this reason, many of us are not happy because we are living in prisons constructed by our limited definitions of our emotions. Don't limit your happiness to what you think defines happiness. Set yourself free, and realize that there are several other feelings and ideas that encompass idle happiness. However, because of our limited definitions, many of us unwisely never consider these feelings and ideas as reasons to be happy. Happiness, like beauty, is defined by the beholder and because we are the beholders, we should behold ourselves as happy.

schema:

body:
- ☐ eat a healthy breakfast.
- ☐ take multivitamins.
- ☐ eat lots of fruits.
- ☐ complete several shoulder presses.
- ☐ complete several calf-raises.

mind:
- ☐ go for a jog.
- ☐ complete several squats.

goals:
- ☐ :
- ☐ :
- ☐ :

reflections:

day thirty - nine:
<u>a cruel world</u>

I finally realized that being grateful to my body was key to giving more love to myself.
Oprah Winfrey (1954 - ****)

When I was about eight years old in Nigeria, I was driving with my father, a plastic and reconstructive surgeon, in heavy traffic. A young man with much scar tissue from burns suddenly approached us, begging for money. Instead of giving him money, my father offered him free surgical treatment for his burns. However, to my surprise, the man politely refused my father's offer. He said that ever since he got burned and started begging, he was making more money to feed his family than he did before his accident, when he worked long grueling hours as a laborer. As a young boy, I failed to understand this man's response, but several years later, I came to realize his honesty and the injustice in our world.

Every time, I think about this man with his extreme facial disfiguration and his refusal to get surgical treatment, I become upset with the corruption and injustice in several parts of the world. However, this feeling makes me extremely grateful for my life. Nowadays, I try not to complain and take things for granted because I know for a fact that my life could be much worse, just like the millions of people around the world trapped in unfortunate circumstances. Sadly, many of us with comfortable lives are quick to complain about petty things. Next time you're about to complain unnecessarily, take a moment to think about all the people like the burnt man who will love or even die to be in your position. There are far more important things in life for anyone to be bogged down with petty stuff. Live every moment with appreciation for life itself.

schema:

body:
- ☐ eat a healthy breakfast.
- ☐ take multivitamins.
- ☐ drink lots of water.
- ☐ complete several push-ups.
- ☐ complete several sit-ups.

mind:
- ☐ appreciate your body.
- ☐ smile and greet everyone.

goals:
- ☐ :
- ☐ :
- ☐ :

reflections:

day forty:
<u>the right attitude</u>

Human beings, by changing the inner attitudes of their minds, can change the outer aspects of their lives.
William James (1842 - 1910)

I define attitude or an attitude as a person's feelings towards any particular aspect of his or her life, and it should come as no surprise that our attitudes affect the world. Our attitudes surround us like an aura, and are capable of directly and indirectly influencing our activities and those of others. Therefore, someone with a positive attitude usually acts positively and positively influences other people, while a negative person gives off negative energy. Nevertheless, I still find it strange that many of us seem forgetful or oblivious to this fact and take our attitudes towards life and towards others for granted.

Children, because of their innocence and apparent sincerity, demonstrate the importance of our attitudes. If you watch a group of children playing, you will notice that their attitude towards each other affects the overall dynamics of the playground. For example, a child with a positive attitude will likely play with others, but a child with a negative attitude will likely start fights with others. It is amazing that one sullen child in a playground can project his or her attitude onto other kids, making them all sullen as well. Have you ever seen a group of kids playing together, when suddenly one child starts to cry and the others begin to cry as well? That's the power of attitude! A positive attitude towards life is the foundation to maintaining a happy life. Always remember to be positive because positive people are happier and usually more successful than negative people.

schema:

body:
- ☐ eat a healthy breakfast.
- ☐ take multivitamins.
- ☐ eat lots of fish.
- ☐ complete several shoulder presses.
- ☐ complete several lunges.

mind:
- ☐ apologize for your faults.
- ☐ relax with music.

goals:
- ☐ :
- ☐ :
- ☐ :

reflections:

epoch four:
isochronal reflections (1)

epoch four:
<u>isochronal reflections (2)</u>

Olusegun 'Sheg' Aranmolate

day forty - one:
<u>added effort</u>

Energy and persistence conquer all things.
   Benjamin Franklin (1706 - 1790)

As a fitness trainer, I often received e-mails from people who wanted the secret to getting into shape and losing weight without exercise. I frankly tell them that no such secret exists, and to ignore diet programs and pills that claim to be the answer. For many of us, getting into shape, like several aspects of our lives, can be more like running a marathon than running a short sprint. If you've ever trained for a marathon, then you know how much focus and endurance that marathons demand. Also, you know that there are times when you want to quit, not because you are a coward, rather because of the grueling nature of a long run.

There are days when life gets tough and we want to quit on ourselves. However, just like long days at work, we must meet the challenge and keep trying. This "never-giving-up" attitude is required to tackle those days when we are confronted with life's challenges. Interestingly, our fast paced lifestyles and desire for instant gratification are often the biggest reasons why many of us fail some of life's challenges. We have forgotten that certain aspects of life require patience and large amounts of time. Come on! You can't pop a pill, go to sleep flabby, and expect to wake up with bulging biceps and washboard abs. Don't be fooled into thinking you can meet life's challenges without the necessary time and effort.

schema:

body:
- ☐ eat a healthy breakfast.
- ☐ take multivitamins.
- ☐ eat lots of fresh salad.
- ☐ play with friends and family.
- ☐ complete several lunges.

mind:
- ☐ laugh at every chance.
- ☐ breathe and introspect.

goals:
- ☐ :
- ☐ :
- ☐ :

reflections:

day forty - two:
<u>flat tires</u>

The only thing that overcomes hard luck is hard work.
Harry Golden (1902 - 1981)

The road to success is like driving on the highway from one town to another. Consequently, many of the rules of the road can be applied to our lives. For example, just like cars on the highway get stalled in traffic at rush-hour, many of us also get stalled at certain points of our lives by several factors that are beyond our control. However, during those times it is important that we remain steadfast and persevere until the road becomes clear. Interestingly, I sometimes have people complain to me about how hard it is to succeed in life, and how the ideas of endurance and perseverance are overrated. It is true that life can get tough and perseverance or endurance can be far from easy, but with the appropriate mindset many of the tough aspects of life can be easier to approach.

Perseverance without motivation is similar to driving a car with flat tires. Any driver should know that flat tires on a car needs to be replaced before it can be driven because the consequences of doing otherwise can be fatal. Likewise, in order for us to persevere through those tough times in life, we need good "motivational tires" to keep us focused and ensure that we don't get stalled during our journey in life. For this reason, it is important that we surround ourselves with good people and positive ideas that continuously motivate and help us strive to the end. Don't be foolish and drive your life with flat tires. If you are stressed out and feel like you're unable to continue your strive through life, it might be a true indicator that you need to take some time off to repair and refill your "motivational tires," so that you don't get involved in a tragic accident in life.

schema:

body:
- ☐ eat a healthy breakfast.
- ☐ take multivitamins.
- ☐ eat lots of steamed vegetable.
- ☐ stretch several times.
- ☐ dance whenever you can.

mind:
- ☐ be kind to everyone.
- ☐ inspire others to change.

goals:
- ☐ :
- ☐ :
- ☐ :

reflections:

day forty - three:
<u>the blueprint</u>

A goal without a plan is just a wish.
Antoine de Saint-Exupery (1900 - 1944)

For many simple things in life, we have a plan or plans for doing them. For instance, we go to the grocery store with the plan to buy groceries and to the mechanic to get our cars fixed. Many of us know from experience that goals without plans to achieve them usually results in failure. For example, if you impulsively walked into the kitchen without a recipe and randomly mixed several foods together into a dish (e.g. bananas, peas, vinegar, tomatoes and sauerkraut), it's unlikely that the dish will be good. It is even more unlikely that you will produce a gourmet dish because gourmet dishes, like several aspects of our lives, require appropriate planning.

Unfortunately, many of us become frustrated with how disorganized we are in achieving our goals. We, however, fail to realize that our lack of plans for the future is the main reason for our woes. Let's be honest with ourselves! How can we ever set things right, if we can't distinguish our left from our right? An important key to becoming successful in life is to set reasonable goals with multiple plans (i.e. plan A, plan B, etc.). It's also crucial that we take time out of our chaotic lives to write our brilliant plans and goals that we want accomplished. Remember that you can't build an architecturally sound house or bridge without a detailed blueprint. Today, make plans to achieve your future goals.

schema:

body:
- ☐ eat a healthy breakfast.
- ☐ take multivitamins.
- ☐ drink lots of fresh juice.
- ☐ complete several bicep curls.
- ☐ complete several standing rows.

mind:
- ☐ meditate.
- ☐ laugh at every chance.

goals:
- ☐ :
- ☐ :
- ☐ :

reflections:

day forty - four:
the privileged ones

The only thing to do with good advice is pass it on. It is never any use to oneself..
Oscar Wilde (1854 - 1900)

Have you ever taken time out of your busy life to appreciate all the wonderful things around you? If you have, then you know that regardless of all the turmoil in the world, there is still much love and affection. If you have not, then you are missing out. The ability to self-reflect is unique to humans, and it's unfortunate that many of us don't use this gift to free ourselves from the stresses of life. Once, I was watching a TV show about people addicted to drugs, and many addicts said that they began using drugs to alleviate their stress. It will be ignorant for anyone to assume that we don't live in a stressful world, but abusing drugs is definitely not the way out. Nevertheless, I hope such people can eventually turn to self-reflection as a way to break their addictions and alleviate stress.

Abusing drugs is similar to placing a bandage over an injury that requires immediate surgery, and if you're familiar with medicine, then you should know that a bandage alone will not do the trick. A good way to start harnessing the power of self-reflection is to think about how blessed you are to simply be alive, especially given all the diseases and other dangers in the world. Think of people in developing countries or those who suffer illnesses like cancer or AIDS. This should really put your blessings in perspective and at least alleviate some stress. Interestingly, in a strange way, the ability for many people to abuse expensive drugs is a privilege and a luxury. Remember, your very existence is a cause for celebration and you should let other people know this fact. Be nice and compassionate to everyone and you will see that there is so much happiness in you.

schema:

body:
- ☐ eat a healthy breakfast.
- ☐ take multivitamins.
- ☐ eat lots of yogurt.
- ☐ go for a jog.
- ☐ complete several sit-ups.

mind:
- ☐ visualize a successful day.
- ☐ think positively.

goals:
- ☐ :
- ☐ :
- ☐ :

reflections:

Olusegun 'Sheg' Aranmolate

day forty - five:
beauty standards

The absence of flaw in beauty is itself a flaw.
Havelock Ellis (1859 - 1939)

It's always heartbreaking to hear beautiful people with so much potential call themselves ugly and worthless. Time and time again, I often try to understand why some people mistreat themselves this way. There is no doubt that we live in an image-conscious society, where people use certain standards and requirements to define beauty. However, because we are human, the truth is that everyone is beautiful, regardless of height, weight, race, or any other characteristic. The words "human" and "being" encompasses so much beauty that it's absurd that some of us constantly subject ourselves to ridiculous standards of beauty.

The ideas of beauty and ugliness are emotional states of mind. For instance, it's very likely that the last time you were angry and happened to look in the mirror, you didn't feel beautiful. It's equally possible that the last time someone complimented you on, say, your hair, you did feel so. But we should not let our emotions determine our sense of beauty. We should break free and appreciate all the beauty emanating from inside us and others. Honestly, why does anyone want to be like the norm? The truth is that if everyone on earth looked like the "perfect" models in the magazine, the world will be a very boring place and there will probably be new standards of beauty. Take a walk around your neighborhood and observe the beauty of diversity in people. People say that beauty is in the eye of the beholder, so when you behold yourself in your mirror, behold yourself as beautiful.

schema:

body:
- ☐ eat a healthy breakfast.
- ☐ take multivitamins.
- ☐ eat lots of fruits.
- ☐ complete several push-ups.
- ☐ play with friends and family.

mind:
- ☐ apologize for your faults.
- ☐ inspire others.

goals:
- ☐ :
- ☐ :
- ☐ :

reflections:

day forty - six:
<u>diamonds forever</u>

Courage and perseverance have a magical talisman, before which difficulties disappear and obstacles vanish into air.
John Quincy Adams (1767 - 1848)

Of course, a well polished diamond has a beautiful luster and shines brilliantly in light. People highly prize diamonds, so they are very expensive. Many people, especially men, even spend fortunes on diamonds and use them as symbols to show their love and affection towards their significant others. In fact, these days, it has almost become a standard requirement for engagement and wedding rings to be encrusted with a piece or pieces of diamonds. Funny enough, many of us are very familiar with the shine of diamonds, but don't know the natural formation process of these brilliant stones.

Diamonds are made in nature from soft opaque carbon, which chemically transforms under high heat and pressure into hard, brown stones. At this point, diamonds look like any ordinary stone. Only after jewelers cut and polish diamonds do they sparkle. Interestingly, the story of most of our lives is similar to the formation of diamonds. The initial stages of our lives are like the opaque carbon that requires intense heat and pressure to be transformed into diamonds. We must realize that difficult times in our lives, like the time carbon spends under high temperature and pressure, are temporary requirements needed to transform ourselves (our mental, physical and emotional states) from one maturity level to the next. Don't fret during these times as they are worth every carat of it!

schema:

body:
- ☐ eat a healthy breakfast.
- ☐ take multivitamins.
- ☐ drink lots of water.
- ☐ complete several sit-ups.
- ☐ go for a walk.

mind:
- ☐ be compassionate to others.
- ☐ apologize for your faults.

goals:
- ☐ :
- ☐ :
- ☐ :

reflections:

day forty - seven:
<u>undetectable essence</u>

While there's life, there's hope.
Cicero (106 BC - 43 BC)

Obviously, we all live in a physical world! Consequently, it's easy for us to simply believe in things we can sense with our sensory organs. For instance, many of us believe in the "seeing is believing" ideology and that if we can't sense a particular thing, then it simply doesn't exist. This way of thinking is false because there are many things or phenomenon that exists in the world that our "rudimentary" sensory organs cannot detect, such as ultra-violet and radio waves. However, over the years, we have learned about their existence because we use them to operate several gadgets. Interestingly, if humans hadn't invented radio receivers to detect the presence of radio waves, technically radio waves wouldn't exist to us.

Many of us need to reevaluate our mentality and realize that there are several things that exist in the world that we cannot detect with our sensory organs. Presently, there isn't a way to quantify or detect genuine human emotions and feelings, such as patience, kindness, compassion, hatred, and even hope. This, however, doesn't disprove their existence and their ability to affect our lives. In fact our emotions and feelings can positively or negatively influence us and others as well, just as invisible magnetic force fields can move metallic objects from a distance. Hence, don't wait for physical proofs before you start practicing and showing others genuine positive human emotions, such as affection, kindness, and compassion. Don't be blinded with your ignorance, and remember that just because you can't detect a human feeling, like hope, doesn't disprove its existence.

schema:

body:
- ☐ eat a healthy breakfast.
- ☐ take multivitamins.
- ☐ eat of vegetables.
- ☐ complete several shoulder presses.
- ☐ complete several calf-raises.

mind:
- ☐ breathe and introspect.
- ☐ plan your future.

goals:
- ☐ :
- ☐ :
- ☐ :

reflections:

day forty - eight:
<u>the laws of time</u>

Time does not change us. It just unfolds us.
  Max Frisch (1911 – 1991)

It should come as no surprise that time governs our lives. From the moment we are born to the moment we die, every aspect of our lives evolves around time. For this reason, we are quick to blame time for many of our problems (like when we say "If only I had enough time"), but fail to acknowledge time for many of our successes. This is similar to the fact that many of us are quick to blame others for our failures in life but are quick to take sole credit for our successes.

The amount of time in a given day is constant and as a result everyone regardless of their creed gets the same amount of time daily. We must realize that we cannot control time and should not take short cuts in life to beat it. In fact, there is some kind of law governing our interactions with time and like any physical law it cannot be violated without consequences. We have all probably heard a story about a person who misses being in a fatal car crash by a few seconds because of a red light. If that person was impatient and tried to run the light to save time, then this person will have arrived in time to be involved in the accident and consequently could have died. Trying to take such short cuts, then, can have very negative consequences. Always be appreciative for every position you find yourself in life, no matter how much "wasted time." Realize that such "wasted time" could be life-savers in disguise and might keep you from trouble, like the person saved by the red light.

schema:

body:
- ☐ eat a healthy breakfast.
- ☐ take multivitamins.
- ☐ eat of fresh juice.
- ☐ complete several sit-ups.
- ☐ complete several squats.

mind:
- ☐ practice patience.
- ☐ be kind to everyone.

goals:
- ☐ :
- ☐ :
- ☐ :

reflections:

Olusegun 'Sheg' Aranmolate

day forty - nine:
ennui

The cure for boredom is curiosity. There is no cure for curiosity.
Dorothy Parker (1893 - 1967)

Wouldn't it be nice to walk barefoot along the shores of a beautiful beach in the morning? What about horseback riding in the woods with a loved one or eating breakfast on an exotic island? These activities are exciting, but unfortunately many of us don't have the time or money to do them. Nevertheless, this is no reason why we can't find other exciting things to do. No matter who you are or where you live, there are good times to be had. Of course, there always will be times in our lives when things feel monotonous or boring. These feelings, however, are normal because we always long for change. They also surely make the exciting times exciting.

We (humans) are clearly different from other animals by our unquenchable desire for change. Consequently, it's not surprising that we often become bored with certain aspects of our lives. Nevertheless, the next time you feel bored, think about the activities that make you feel alive and then find affordable ways to engage in those activities. For instance, as a child a couple friends and I really liked and enjoyed playing soccer, but at times when we couldn't find soccer balls, we made substitutes out of banana leaves. You might be surprised that a little change or substitution is all you need to get you out of ennui (a state of boredom). Keep in mind, however, that simply because an activity makes you feel excited doesn't mean that it's good for you. This is because several self-destructive activities might seem exciting. Be smart with your choices, have fun, and remember that you don't have to be rich to live an exciting life.

schema:

body:
- [ ] eat a healthy breakfast.
- [ ] take multivitamins.
- [ ] eat lots of seafood.
- [ ] dance whenever you can.
- [ ] stretch several times.

mind:
- [ ] apologize for your faults.
- [ ] compliment others.

goals:
- [ ] :
- [ ] :
- [ ] :

reflections:

day fifty:
<u>the successful mistake</u>

Success is the ability to go from one failure to another with no loss of enthusiasm.
    Sir Winston Churchill (1874 - 1965)

A few decades ago, if a deep cut on your leg got infected, then you had a high chance of getting an amputation or dying from shock. However, all this changed with the discovery of Penicillin, which Sir Alexander Fleming accidentally discovered in 1928. At the time, he was working with some bacteria cultures and discovered that a foreign organism had contaminated them. Quickly, however, he realized the contaminant—now called Penicillin—was killing the bacteria. Since this lucky discovery, Penicillin has saved millions of lives and is still used today in the fight against many disease-causing bacteria.

This story is inspirational because it reveals that sometimes mistakes turn out to be great accomplishments. Sadly, however, many of us may miss these occurrences because society teaches us to like or celebrate our successes, but to dislike or ignore our failures. If Sir Fleming did that, then, the world will have missed out on a great discovery. It is worth noting, however, that our definitions of success and failure are subjective! We usually view success as instances when we get "expected results" and failure as instances when we don't. As a result, many of us continually feel like failures because we expect the "wrong results" from life and unwisely consider many of our successes as failures. Be more attentive to your mistakes and try to learn something from them. You never know, your next mistake might turnout to be your greatest accomplishment in life.

schema:

body:

- ☐ eat a healthy breakfast.
- ☐ take multivitamins.
- ☐ eat lots of yogurt.
- ☐ go for a jog.
- ☐ complete several sit-ups.

mind:

- ☐ cherish today like it's your last.
- ☐ inspire others.

goals:

- ☐ :
- ☐ :
- ☐ :

reflections:

Olusegun 'Sheg' Aranmolate

epoch five:
isochronal reflections (1)

epoch five:
isochronal reflections (2)

day fifty - one:
manipulative

Ninety-nine percent of all failures come from people who
have the habit of making excuses.
George Washington Carver (1864 – 1943)

While I was in college, I attended several campus debates.
Fellow students would argue about many topics, such as
bioethics, politics, and pop-culture. These debates were
educative and I learned that smart people with the right words
can sell a weak point to any audience. During one debate, I
remember watching a young man argue his way out of a
position that I thought was relatively weak and effortlessly
defeat his opponent with his cunning use of the English
vocabulary. We all must realize that, just like this young man, we
are capable of manipulating words and providing
rationalization in defense of negative actions and behaviors.

Let's be honest with ourselves. If we are defending a negative
behavior or position through rationalization, then we are clearly
engaging in deception—self-deception. For example I have
heard some people tell me that they are a "little-bit" hateful or
a "little-bit" hurtful and as a result they are not hateful or hurtful
people. The truth, however, is that positive or negative human
behaviors and feelings can't be quantified. Therefore, a person
can't be a "little-bit" hateful or a "little-bit" hurtful. If you have a
little bit of hate or a lot of hate, the bottom-line is that you are
hateful. Remember that just as different people have different
pain thresholds, different people also have different emotional
thresholds. Hence, what you might consider to be a little bit of
hate might be perceived by someone else as the greatest form
of hate possible. Stop the denial and be considerate with your
words and your actions because like weapons they can be
used for good or evil.

schema:

body:
- ☐ eat a healthy breakfast.
- ☐ take multivitamins.
- ☐ eat lots of steamed vegetables.
- ☐ take the stairs, instead of the elevator.
- ☐ complete several standing rows.

mind:
- ☐ prioritize your life.
- ☐ appreciate yourself.

goals:
- ☐ :
- ☐ :
- ☐ :

reflections:

day fifty - two:
jam-packed

Do not anticipate trouble, or worry about what may never happen. Keep in the sunlight.
  Benjamin Franklin (1706 – 1790)

Have you ever noticed the large amounts of stuff that some people have in their basements and garages? Once, I was helping a family clean out their garage because it was disorganized and could no longer fit a car. As I started cleaning, I discovered that there was a larger ratio of junk to valuable items all stacked together, giving it all a poor appearance. The family's overcrowded garage revealed a unique desire of some humans to continuously acquire and accumulate things. This habit could have dated back to the stone ages, when we needed to save things to survive, but who knows? Nevertheless, the truth is that, over time, these acquired items can crowd our lives.

Interestingly, many of our minds—filled with both junky and valuable ideas—can become like overstocked garages. Our junky ideas, such as thoughts of envy, racism, and superiority, can even end up crowding out our many great ideas, making it difficult to access great ideas when we need them. For instance, will you be able to truly help the less-fortunate, when your mind is filled with thoughts of superiority? Or, comically, will you want to discuss serious political issues with references to your favorite childhood video game? Don't let those valuable thoughts of yours become overshadowed by worthless and junky ideas. Today, clean out your mind, ditch junky ideas, and fill your head with good ideas. Don't be a junk collector! Set yourself free from habitual junk collecting.

schema:

body:

- ☐ eat a healthy breakfast.
- ☐ take multivitamins.
- ☐ drink lots of green tea.
- ☐ stretch several times.
- ☐ complete several shoulder presses.

mind:

- ☐ relax with music.
- ☐ laugh at every chance.

goals:

- ☐ :
- ☐ :
- ☐ :

reflections:

day fifty - three:
the exaggerator

The visionary lies to himself, the liar only to others.
Friedrich Nietzsche (1844 - 1900)

When many people think of great storytellers, they usually think of renowned novelists and authors who have written bestselling books. However, when I think about great storytellers, I think of children. Have you ever heard a child tell a story about a normal event, such a trip to the supermarket or a birthday party? If so, then I bet at least parts of the story were beyond belief. Once a boy told me about a birthday party he attended where the cake was bigger than a car. Of course, I knew the boy was exaggerating about the huge cake, but, not wanting to quell his excitement, I played along and acted amazed.

Even as adults, there are times when we exaggerate stories for our friends and family. This makes sense, as people often enjoy listening to exaggerations, which make things more interesting. In story-telling situations, exaggerations, then, can be acceptable distortions of the truth. However, we must realize that exaggerating facts is basically lying. Therefore, listeners may come to distrust those who are in the habit of exaggerating stories. If you are a chronic exaggerator, don't be surprised if others disbelieve your stories or other things you say, even when you are telling the truth. During our everyday lives and when telling stories, it is important to emphasize the most entertaining aspects of the story without exaggerating the truth. Don't always cry wolf when there are no wolves around because when the wolves truly arrive, no one will be there for the "exaggerator."

schema:

body:
- ☐ eat a healthy breakfast.
- ☐ take multivitamins.
- ☐ eat lots of fruits.
- ☐ go for a walk.
- ☐ complete several sit-ups.

mind:
- ☐ visualize a successful day.
- ☐ smile and greet everyone today.

goals:
- ☐ :
- ☐ :
- ☐ :

reflections:

day fifty - four:
<u>deceiving looks</u>

All generalizations are dangerous, even this one.
Alexandre Dumas (1802 - 1870)

We are all familiar with the saying "never judge a book by its cover"? Over the years, I have read some great books with terrible covers, and I have also read some terrible books with great covers. Obviously, we live an image-conscious world, where so many of us tend to make large generalizations based solely on what we observe. This ability to make guesses and generalizations based on what we see might have helped our ancestors survive various poisonous plants and deadly animals but, in current times, this ability is no longer so helpful, at least in regards to generalizing people.

Honestly, if only many of us took the time to better understand our friends and lovers, rather than being taken by their physical appearance alone, many of us would and could have avoided being involved in hurtful relationships. I am not in any way suggesting that we shouldn't appreciate beauty or beautiful people, but such appreciation should never be the main factor for our choices and decisions. Clearly, it will be ludicrous for someone to purchase a pretty or sleek-looking car without making sure it has a functional engine. Similarly, why get involved in a relationship without understanding your partner and making sure you are both compatible? Be attentive and don't be fooled by appearance alone because to a large extent looks can truly be misleading.

schema:

body:
- ☐ eat a healthy breakfast.
- ☐ take multivitamins.
- ☐ drink lots of water.
- ☐ complete several calf-raises.
- ☐ complete several lunges.

mind:
- ☐ breathe and introspect.
- ☐ laugh at every chance.

goals:
- ☐ :
- ☐ :
- ☐ :

reflections:

Olusegun 'Sheg' Aranmolate

day fifty - five:
<u>the sculptor</u>

One of the most important lessons that experience teaches is that, on the whole, success depends more upon character than upon either intellect or fortune.
William Edward Hartpole Lecky (1838-1903)

If you ever met a person who was saved from drowning by a rescue dog, then it's very likely that this person will be caring towards dogs. In contrast, if this same person was attacked by a dog instead of being rescued, then it's very likely that this person will fear and dislike dogs. It is astounding to realize that a lot of our ideas, behaviors, and choices are shaped by our various life experiences. Suppose you gave a skilled and an amateur sculptor some clay and told them each to make a statue of an angel, it is likely that the skilled sculptor will do a better job. However, if the skilled sculptor was given dried clay while the amateur was given fresh clay, then it's more likely that the amateur will come out on top.

In comparison to our lives, our environments are like the sculptors, capable of shaping us into good or bad angels. A nurturing environment is like a skilled sculptor and a difficult environment is like an amateur sculptor. The difference is that we are not like pieces of clay—we have our own personalities and can get motivated to change, and this can ultimately determine the way our environments shape us. If you are currently in a difficult environment, don't be discouraged. If you are, then your environment can or might shape you negatively. Just think about all the successful people in the world who were once in conditions similar to yours. Always remain tough and steadfast in difficult situations so that you force your environment to shape you in positive ways.

schema:

body:
- ☐ eat a healthy breakfast.
- ☐ take multivitamins.
- ☐ eat lots of fresh fish.
- ☐ play with friends and family.
- ☐ cook a delicious meal.

mind:
- ☐ meditate.
- ☐ think positively.

goals:
- ☐ :
- ☐ :
- ☐ :

reflections:

day fifty - six:
the hiker's pack

Nothing endures but change.
Heraclitus (540 BC - 480 BC)

I have gone hiking in the woods a couple times. For me, hiking is a meditative and invigorating activity that allows my body to exercise and my mind to relax. From experience, I can confidently say that having the correct hiking gear is necessary and it can be the difference between having a safe, enjoyable hike or a dangerous and miserable one. There are certain essential items that every hiker should have during a hiking trip, such as a good sleeping bag, water bottle, canned food items, utensils, and maybe a book or two. However, to make hiking easier it's important to take only essential items because carrying a heavy back-pack can become unbearable after hiking for a few miles.

As time goes on while hiking, most backpacks, regardless of how lightly packed, become heavier and heavier. However, a hiker can't simply throw away his or her back pack to lessen the burden because the pack is the hiker's means of survival in the woods. Our journey through life is like hiking. Our everyday obligations, such as our jobs and taking care of family members, are like the essential items in a hiker's back-pack. Similar to how hikers should not toss away their back-packs, we should never desert our jobs or family members. However, when our schedules become too busy and we become overwhelmed with life, it's wise only for us to give up activities that are not essential to our responsibilities and health e.g. worrying about the latest celebrity gossip or downloading new songs. Don't overwhelm yourself with superfluous activities and hold onto the important things in life.

schema:

body:
- ☐ eat a healthy breakfast.
- ☐ take multivitamins.
- ☐ eat lots of fresh salad.
- ☐ go for a jog.
- ☐ complete several sit-ups.

mind:
- ☐ talk less and listen more.
- ☐ be grateful.

goals:
- ☐ :
- ☐ :
- ☐ :

reflections:

day fifty - seven:
our reputation

A good reputation is more valuable than money.
  Publilius Syrus (100 BC)

One day, my friend called and described how he just bought a brand new car. I immediately asked him to tell me more about his car—the brand, the model and the specifications. My friend proudly answered my questions and told me all the details of his new ride. Upon hearing his answer, I quickly realized why my friend was so excited and proud of his luxurious import. All of us are familiar with brand name products and logos because we are surrounded by them, and because many of the products we use daily are branded with some unique logo. From experience and from watching advertisements we have learned to attach value, quality, and even price to items based on their logos. For instance, many of us can see the logo of a car company and estimate the value, price, and reputation of the company's cars.

Our mannerisms and behaviors are very much like logos, and just like we use logos to determine the quality of a product, other people use our manners and behaviors to judge our character. If you ever had a bad experience with a company, it is likely that this experience will cause you to dislike the company, their products, and even their logos. As a result, every time you see that company's logo, you might be reminded of your bad experience. Similarly, many of us have damaged our character, or at least the image people have of it, by acting inappropriately or by having obnoxious manners. Remember that your reputation belongs to you and it's your responsibility to preserve it. Uphold your reputation like it's your most precious belonging— it's extremely difficult to repair a tarnished image.

schema:

body:
- ☐ eat a healthy breakfast.
- ☐ take multivitamins.
- ☐ drink lots of green tea.
- ☐ complete several standing rows.
- ☐ stretch several times.

mind:
- ☐ take a mental vacation.
- ☐ smile and greet everyone.

goals:
- ☐ :
- ☐ :
- ☐ :

reflections:

day fifty - eight:
<u>diversification</u>

If we cannot end now our differences, at least we can help make the world safe for diversity.
John F. Kennedy (1917 - 1963)

Suppose a total stranger asked you why you cherished and enjoyed life, will you be able to give a genuine answer to this question? Honestly, I personally will have a tough time answering such a question because there are too many aspects of life that I cherish. Nevertheless, if I was forced to give an answer, I will say that I cherish and enjoy life because of the beautiful diversity in the world. Clearly, many of us go to the zoo to see exotic animals that we normally don't encounter in our everyday lives. Now, suppose you and your family went to the zoo and after paying the entrance fee, discovered that the entire zoo was populated with only cows. I am quite sure that you will be disappointed and might even demand a refund.

It is surprising, then, that many of us are intolerant of human diversity and differences in other people. Certainly, many of us prefer to live around others with similar beliefs, interests, and lifestyles. We also tend to believe that our lifestyles are the best and should be the standard for others. However, we must remember that if everyone in our society was the same (dressed, looked, spoke, and acted the same), then our society will be less interesting and beautiful than it is now. Diversity makes our world an interestingly beautiful place! Don't be a closed minded individual—embrace the diversity of persons around you, including their ideas, appearance, culture, musical interests, etc. You will be surprised that such a change will allow you to cherish your time on this beautiful planet that we all consider home.

schema:

body:
- ☐ eat a healthy breakfast.
- ☐ take multivitamins.
- ☐ eat lots of fruits.
- ☐ go for a walk.
- ☐ complete several squats.

mind:
- ☐ be kind to everyone.
- ☐ be grateful.

goals:
- ☐ :
- ☐ :
- ☐ :

reflections:

Olusegun 'Sheg' Aranmolate

day fifty - nine:
emotional projections

You must learn from the mistakes of others. You can't possibly
live long enough to make them all yourself.
Sam Levenson (1911 - 1980)

Late one night, while I was studying for an important
biochemistry exam, a lady friend of mine called me and was
sobbing because she had just broken up with her boyfriend. She
desperately needed my help, so, forgetting my exam, I focused
my attention on her and talked to her. As we began talking, I
was surprised to hear her anger and resentment toward her
boyfriend because there was a time when they were literally
inseparable from one another. Luckily, after talking to her for
about two hours, she relaxed and felt better about her situation.

Humans are very interesting creatures and it is amazing how
fast our feelings and attitude towards a person can change
from love to dislike in a matter of seconds. When we really like a
person, we become excited to be around him or her and
everything always seems perfect. For instance, when that
person tells a story, we are attentive and quick to laugh at the
person's jokes, even when the jokes aren't funny. However,
when we dislike a person, everything he or she does puts us on
edge. Even simple things like the way the person talks, walks, or
even smiles can annoy us. The reason for this drastic change is
that our emotions largely depend on the actions of other
people and in return we project our emotions on others. Thus,
our anger towards people who hurt us reveals itself through our
actions and the way we perceive them. Many of us could be
less angry with ourselves and with others, if we reflected on how
we are letting our emotions affect our perception of the world.
Nevertheless, avoid getting involved in relationships with people
who act badly—they will evenly hurt you.

schema:

body:

- ☐ eat a healthy breakfast.
- ☐ take multivitamins.
- ☐ drink lots of water.
- ☐ play with friends and family.
- ☐ dance whenever you can.

mind:

- ☐ prioritize your life.
- ☐ meditate.

goals:

- ☐ :
- ☐ :
- ☐ :

reflections:

Olusegun 'Sheg' Aranmolate

day sixty:
<u>cute skunks</u>

I was always looking outside myself for strength and confidence, but it comes from within. It is there all the time.
Anna Freud (1895 - 1982)

Skunks are famous for their ability to spray a chemical so potent that it makes large predators run away in disgust. The truth, however, is that skunks usually release this potent scent at times when they are scared or feel threatened by potentially dangerous animals. Nevertheless, besides their intense smell, skunks are actually cute animals. Take a look at several pictures of skunks in the library or online, and you may be surprised to realize that their small heads, petite bodies, and fluffy black and white fur makes them really adorable.

Interestingly, many people are like these adorable skunks. Such people are usually, at first meeting, attractive, nice and cordial. However, as soon as people try to get close to them, they become anxious, show their nasty side, and push others away with their distant behaviors. This erratic behavior is usually due to painful experiences in life that have made such people inherently distrusting of others. Ironically, many of these people don't always realize that they are actually pushing others away and wonder why they can't be in stable relationships. Don't be like a cute skunk that lures people with looks, only to treat them poorly and spray them with harsh manners. Learn to understand yourself and other people before making any assumptions so that you don't chase away great people from your life.

schema:

body:

- ☐ eat a healthy breakfast.
- ☐ take multivitamins.
- ☐ eat lots of steamed vegetable.
- ☐ cook a delicious meal.
- ☐ complete several squats.

mind:

- ☐ think positively.
- ☐ laugh at every chance.

goals:

- ☐ :
- ☐ :
- ☐ :

reflections:

epoch six:
<u>isochronal reflections (1)</u>

epoch six:
<u>isochronal reflections (2)</u>

day sixty - one:
<u>the connoisseur</u>

The wisest mind has something yet to learn.
George Santayana (1863 - 1952)

You may have once heard that "to walk, one must first learn to crawl." This old adage, despite its simplicity, embodies a powerful message, which is that to become proficient in any skill, even one as complex as performing brain surgery, a person must begin as a novice and work up to the proficiency level of an expert. Have you ever thought about how it took several years for us to learn to walk correctly and write without making a mess? Isn't it ironic, then, that many of us are impatient when it comes to learning new ideas and achieving success.

The reason many of us fail in trying to start or do new things is that we have already given up on ourselves, even before we started. Obviously, achieving any form of success isn't an easy task. Nevertheless, enduring through tough times is necessary for us to achieve our goals. What will happen if babies around the world suddenly stopped trying to walk? Such an event will be a cause for alarm and will be catastrophic to the human race. Fortunately, babies don't give up and they continually push themselves to get on their own feet—they fall several times but keep pushing until they become successful. Don't be fooled by get-rich schemes or fad-diets. Success, like any skill, requires sacrifice and dedication. Remember that you didn't learn to walk overnight, so don't expect to manifest all your desires overnight, either.

schema:

body:
- ☐ eat a healthy breakfast.
- ☐ take multivitamins.
- ☐ eat lots of yogurt.
- ☐ complete several bench dips.
- ☐ complete several shoulder presses.

mind:
- ☐ cherish today like it's your last.
- ☐ meditate.

goals:
- ☐ :
- ☐ :
- ☐ :

reflections:

day sixty - two:
a statistic

There are three kinds of lies: lies, damned lies, and statistics.
Benjamin Disraeli (1804 - 1881)

Companies make billions of dollars in profit yearly on fitness and weight-loss programs, while the United States government spends billions on weight-related issues. However, despite all the profits made and all the money spent, the United States Centers for Disease Control and Prevention estimates that more than half of Americans are overweight, of which more than half are obese. Unquestionably, there are several health problems associated with being overweight, such as diabetes, chronic fatigue, brittle bones, breathlessness, and other issues. I find it particularly disturbing to realize that many people on a daily basis are subjected to these debilitating conditions. Of course, there are some people whose weight issues are due to their genetic makeup, but a larger percentage of people are overweight simply due to bad eating habits

It is normal for humans to want to overeat when we have access to a plethora of cheap food, but the effect will often be weight gain. Honestly, have you ever seen an overweight person in those documentaries about famine in other countries? These people are usually extremely thin and bony. However, if these famished individuals were given unlimited access to fatty foods, then many of them will overeat and consequently become overweight. The function of food is to provide us with the correct nutrients required to function properly, but presently many of us have become habitual eaters who eat simply for enjoyment or for the sake of eating. If you do this, then you can't keep blaming food for your weight problem. We all have free will and can avoid overeating. Don't let yourself become a statistic for weight gain. Stop making excuses! Exercise free will and start living a healthy lifestyle.

schema:

body:
- ☐ eat a healthy breakfast.
- ☐ take multivitamins.
- ☐ eat some chocolate.
- ☐ cook a delicious meal.
- ☐ complete several sit-ups.

mind:
- ☐ breathe and introspect.
- ☐ appreciate your day.

goals:
- ☐ :
- ☐ :
- ☐ :

reflections:

day sixty - three:
true fairy tales

Rarely do great beauty and great virtue dwell together.
Francesco Petrarch (1304 - 1374)

Cinderella, *Sleeping Beauty*, and several other fairy tales are inspirational because they teach children and adults, alike, the triumphant power of good over evil. Interestingly, the story and life of Cinderella has a strong correlation to the lives of many of us today. According to the tale, Cinderella was of a noble bloodline, but with the death of her father, her family status was reduced. Consequently, Cinderella was forced to become a maid and slave for her evil stepmother. Despite all her adversaries, she remained kindhearted and optimistic that her situation will someday improve. Fortunately, after various trials and tribulations, Cinderella came out victorious and lived happily ever after with her Prince Charming.

Many of us, like Cinderella, are meant to be living successful lives, but, due to unfortunate circumstances, have been unable to improve our situations. We try really hard to climb up the ladder of life, but it always seems like an evil stepmother is thwarting our plans. Then, unexpectedly, like the appearance of the fairy godmother, we encounter a promising opportunity that changes our lives for the better. However, just like Cinderella forgot about the time limit of the fairy godmother's spell, many of us get so carried away by all the glamour of our new lives that we forget our true values, only to be relegated to our previously tough lives. Unlike many of us who will immediately lose hope upon relegation, Cinderella didn't lose faith and in no time was back in the palace. Interestingly, she didn't even have to look for success because success (in form of the Prince) came looking for her. Don't lose hope if your life is looking bleak. Your redemption might just be around the corner, looking frantically for you, like the Prince searching for the lady with the glass slipper.

schema:

body:
- ☐ eat a healthy breakfast.
- ☐ take multivitamins.
- ☐ eat lots of fruits.
- ☐ complete several push-ups.
- ☐ complete several squats.

mind:
- ☐ inspire people to change.
- ☐ smile and greet everyone today.

goals:
- ☐ :
- ☐ :
- ☐ :

reflections:

day sixty - four:
different angles

> If there is any one secret of success, it lies in the ability to get the other person's point of view and see things from that person's angle as well as from your own.
> Henry Ford (1863-1947)

Whenever I watch a movie on DVD, I enjoy watching the movie blurbs, the "behind-the-scenes" footage, and the director's cuts. These clips take away the larger-than-life feel of most movies and often reveal the true personalities of the performers. Interestingly, most directors mention that they re-shoot certain scenes several times not because of bad lighting or poor acting from the performers, but to get different angles of the same scene, which gives audiences a dynamic view of the acting.

We should apply the rationale of directors to re-shoot scenes to our own lives. For example, many of us think that we are living uneventful lives. This is not because we are boring but because we tend to view our lives with a narrow focus. Thus, we miss many of the important details that make life worthwhile, like how our advice has helped, say, our younger siblings or how your idea in class gave someone else a different perspective on life. We also tend to become impatient and upset when we feel that we are stalled in life or that we are repeating certain aspects of our lives again (e.g. summer school or a difficult class). However, similar to a great movie director repeating certain scenes for quality reasons, being stalled or having to repeat certain aspects of our lives can be a golden opportunity for us to get a better view of our lives and what goals we want to pursue. Treat your life as a vigilant director will treat his or her movie.

schema:

body:
- ☐ eat a healthy breakfast.
- ☐ take multivitamins.
- ☐ eat lots of steamed vegetables.
- ☐ complete several bicep curls.
- ☐ complete several bench dips.

mind:
- ☐ compliment others.
- ☐ think positively.

goals:
- ☐ :
- ☐ :
- ☐ :

reflections:

Olusegun 'Sheg' Aranmolate

day sixty - five:
a little donation

The strongest principle of growth lies in human choice.
George Eliot (1819 - 1880)

One day Mark, one of my closest friends, called from Rwanda, where he had been working for several months with doctors in a hospital. I was excited to hear my friend and wanted to know about his experiences in Africa. Because of the tragic acts of genocide that occurred there in 1994, I expected to hear horrifying stories about this country. However, to my surprise most of his stories were pretty exciting and interesting. He told me about hikes he took in the rainforest, his safari in Kenya, and his encounter with lions and several other exotic animals. He also mentioned how, in recent weeks, he had lost a couple pounds. This was surprising to hear because he is pretty skinny. He told me that, when he arrived at the village and saw many hungry children, he had decided to give one of his meals each day to a hungry family or a child. Mark said that it was exhilarating to make such a simple sacrifice for so great an effect.

Mark's description of his days in Rwanda was very touching. It also made me think about the attitude many people have about fitness and weight loss. In developed countries, people have access to large amounts of food and some go on strict and often excessively restricting diets to lose some extra pounds. I realized that, if everyone in America and other developed countries who are on a diet acted like my friend and gave a meal a day to less fortunate individuals or the money equivalent to meal to a non-profit organization, then both parties (the givers and the receivers) could benefit greatly.

schema:

body:
- ☐ eat a healthy breakfast.
- ☐ take multivitamins.
- ☐ drink lots of water.
- ☐ complete several push-ups.
- ☐ complete several sit-ups.

mind:
- ☐ laugh at every chance.
- ☐ smile and greet everyone today.

goals:
- ☐ :
- ☐ :
- ☐ :

reflections:

day sixty - six:
<u>opinionated folks</u>

Everyone rises to their level of incompetence.
Laurence J. Peter (1919 - 1988)

Nowadays, we can't watch television without seeing at least one car commercial, featuring the latest gadgets and gizmos of newer models. It is undeniable that the great angle shots of the cars, along with the electrifying background music in these commercials, usually makes the average viewer crave newer models. A vintage car collector, however, might not be intrigued by these commercials. In fact, such a person might consider these commercials as tacky and tasteless. The truth is that different people have different tastes, views, and opinions for the same thing. Thus, what you might consider to be absolutely appealing might be absolutely repulsive to someone else, and vice-versa.

Interestingly, it seems like many of us have become oblivious to our differences in taste that so often we try to subject our opinions on others, and will sometimes become upset when others don't agree with our opinions. Many people, especially the youngsters, are frustrated with their lives, mainly because their family members and friends want them to live according to certain standards. It can be particularly annoying, when it seems like everyone around you is trying to subject their ideas upon you, while disregarding your ideas. However, you need to realize that no one, but yourselves, can truly know how it feels like to be you, and how you are affected by certain opinions. Therefore, it's important that you always have a final say in opinions that affect your live. Don't become someone else's puppet, take control of your own strings, and realize that you are entitled to your own unique taste.

schema:

body:
- ☐ eat a healthy breakfast.
- ☐ take multivitamins.
- ☐ eat lots of seafood.
- ☐ go for a walk.
- ☐ stretch several times.

mind:
- ☐ practice tolerance.
- ☐ cherish today like it's your last.

goals:
- ☐ :
- ☐ :
- ☐ :

reflections:

Olusegun 'Sheg' Aranmolate

day sixty - seven:
unfamiliar territory

Change your thoughts and you change your world.
Norman Vincent Peale (1898 - 1993)

When I first learned that I was going to the United States for college, I was excited about the prospect of being independent and free from my parent's control. However, when I first arrived and saw the large campus, I immediately became nervous and nostalgic. I realized that I was far away from home and in unfamiliar territory. Nevertheless, I knew that there was no turning back— I had to adjust to my new environment. The truth about many of us is that we get excited about the idea of changing certain aspects of our lives, but become fearful and apprehensive when these changes occur.

In life, change is inevitable and although necessary can be difficult and painful. For example, every child at some point has to painfully lose their baby teeth for stronger permanent teeth, college graduates have to adjust to the work world, and young parents have to deal with the new demands and challenges of parenthood. However, by being positive and with determination, life changes can make us stronger and better individuals. Think about it! Humans are resilient by nature and, in time, we can adapt to almost any environment. If you are going through changes in your life that seem unbearable, realize that things will get better. You're a member of the resilient human race, which, in efforts to explore and adapt to new environments, has moved mountains, redirected rivers, built submarines, and designed spaceships, simply by changing and applying their thoughts.

schema:

body:

- ☐ eat a healthy breakfast.
- ☐ take multivitamins.
- ☐ drink lots of water.
- ☐ complete several push-ups.
- ☐ complete several lunges.

mind:

- ☐ be grateful.
- ☐ be compassionate to others.

goals:

- ☐ :
- ☐ :
- ☐ :

reflections:

Olusegun 'Sheg' Aranmolate

day sixty - eight:
<u>trepidation</u>

Mistakes are the portals of discovery.
James Joyce (1882 - 1941)

As a youngster, I was so fond of martial arts that I often acted out scenes from the many martial arts movies I saw. Over the years, I concluded that most of these movies were about a defeated underdog who, after undergoing rigorous training, became victorious in the end. These movies, besides their intense action scenes and sometimes humorous dialogues, taught valuable lessons about the importance of perseverance and the crippling effects of fear. For example, one movie showed how an inexperienced fighter could meditate and train hard enough to beat an expert killer who had enslaved the fighter's village and who had once almost beaten the fighter to death.

Many of us face times of great trial and tribulation, such as when we battle deadly addictions, lose our jobs, become bankrupt, fall gravely ill, or lose a loved one. These moments can be frightening and can test our willpower. However, the difference between getting through these times and giving up can often be our ability to persevere, which involves controlling our fears. Fear truly has a crippling effect on us! It makes us hesitate and we become vulnerable to making mistakes. Don't allow your fears to prevent you from getting the upper hand in life. Next time you face a difficult situation that seems to test your might, relax, think logically and control your fears. In the end, you might be surprised that it is a lot easier to sail through tough times.

schema:

body:
- ☐ eat a healthy breakfast.
- ☐ take multivitamins.
- ☐ eat lots of steamed vegetable.
- ☐ stretch several times.
- ☐ complete several squats.

mind:
- ☐ be patient.
- ☐ apologize for your faults.

goals:
- ☐ :
- ☐ :
- ☐ :

reflections:

day sixty - nine:
<u>crappy roommate</u>

Be modest! It is the kind of pride least likely to offend.
Jules Renard (1864 - 1910)

In graduate school, I instructed an introductory biology lab for undergraduates. I noticed that one of my students was particularly upset, so, at the end of one class, I asked her how things were going. It turned out that she was upset with her roommate, who was particularly nasty and arrogant towards her. I understood why she could be down— it can be miserable living with an inhospitable person. I told her, trying to give advice, that rather than becoming so upset in dealing with her roommate, she should act nicely. A week later, my student thanked me for this advice and said that she felt better acting this way. Her roommate, she went on, would even get upset by her kindness. Hopefully, her roommate eventually learned from my student's example.

Many of us fail to realize that we often subconsciously try to impose our state of mind on others around us. For instance, when a person is happy, he or she usually wants to spread this happiness to others. When that person is sad or upset, however, he or she may want to bring others down. If we are around someone in the latter case, we should remind ourselves that no one should be able to ruin our day. The world is filled with so many daunting issues—we could use our attention for positive things, such as feeding starving children, assisting the elderly, and helping the less-fortunate. We can't always control the way other people feel, but we can control how we feel and deal with those people. Try to treat someone who is treating you poorly with kindness. If all else fails, walk away. Just don't let someone make you act nasty. Nevertheless, always try to enjoy life and be a dispenser of joy rather than hatred.

schema:

body:
- ☐ eat a healthy breakfast.
- ☐ take multivitamins.
- ☐ drink lots of fresh juice.
- ☐ complete several shoulder presses.
- ☐ complete several squats.

mind:
- ☐ take mental vacation.
- ☐ compliment others.

goals:
- ☐ :
- ☐ :
- ☐ :

reflections:

day seventy:
<u>true junkies</u>

Fight for your opinions, but do not believe that they contain the whole truth, or the only truth.
Charles A. Dana (1819 - 1897)

Many of us have become so addicted to coffee that we literally can't start our days without some. When we think about addicts, we usually think about drug addicts—rarely those addicted to coffee. An addiction is basically a condition in which someone compulsively occupies his or her time with a substance or some activity. Thus, some addicts include sport fanatics, workaholics, and even party animals. Interestingly, many of us fall into one of the above categories, and it is ironic that we can be quick to judge other addicts and act like we're flawless.

Philosophically, there is little difference between, say, a coffee addict and a cocaine addict because both individuals are dependent on a substance for a stimulus. To better understand drug addicts, we should keep in mind that if some evil-doer forcibly injected some people with a drug like cocaine, then many of them will probably develop an addiction to the substance. Given this, we should be more tolerant and not judge people who have become addicted to drugs, although we should tell addicts that they have made a grave mistake and we should help them recover. Realize that we all have flaws and are all capable of making mistakes, just like drug addicts made a grave mistake. It's better to help addicts off their addiction than waste time judging and criticizing. If you know someone is addicted to a bad substance or activity, help them.

schema:

body:
- ☐ eat a healthy breakfast.
- ☐ take multivitamins.
- ☐ eat some chocolate.
- ☐ stretch several times.
- ☐ cook a delicious meal.

mind:
- ☐ relax with music.
- ☐ be kind to everyone.

goals:
- ☐ :
- ☐ :
- ☐ :

reflections:

epoch seven:
isochronal reflections (1)

epoch seven:
<u>isochronal reflections (2)</u>

day seventy - one:
set the rules

Laughter gives us distance. It allows us to step back from an event, deal with it and then move on.
Bob Newhart (1929 - ****)

There's no doubt that you will be out of place if you wore swim trunks to graduation or a tuxedo on a camping trip. We live in a society with fashion rules for different occasions. In many situations, there can be some flexibility to what we can wear. For instance, we can wear almost anything, from a dress shirt to jeans, at a beach party. Nevertheless, the reason we set fashion standards is to prevent our lives from getting mundane and to ensure that we feel special when we dress elaborately. If everyone wore the same clothes all the time, no matter the event, sooner or later our lives will become dull. However, unlike with types of dress in certain situations, we should never treat people with different levels of dignity.

It is illogical that many of us have silly rules regarding the way we interact with people. For example, I had a friend who, back in college, used to be nice to everyone. However, after graduating and getting a job, he became cold and distant towards people. This was probably due to his false perception that older, working-class individuals are supposed to be serious and unfriendly. Obviously, we undergo several behavioral changes as we age and mature, but this shouldn't be a reason to become arrogant or mean-spirited. Life is hard enough! Just like humans need food to live, we need laughter to help us survive our stressful society. Break the cycle of acting so differently to different people—laugh and don't worry about others laughing at you because if everyone was laughing no one will be fighting.

schema:

body:
- ☐ eat a healthy breakfast.
- ☐ take multivitamins.
- ☐ eat lots of fish.
- ☐ complete several sit-ups.
- ☐ complete several squats.

mind:
- ☐ apologize for your faults.
- ☐ compliment others.

goals:
- ☐ :
- ☐ :
- ☐ :

reflections:

Olusegun 'Sheg' Aranmolate

day seventy - two:
<u>precious ideas</u>

This is my answer to the gap between ideas and action - I will write it out.
Hortense Calisher (1911 - ****)

I was up late one night in college working frantically on a physics assignment due the next day. One of the physics problems was particularly challenging and I spent several hours trying to figure it out. Suddenly, I thought of the solution but, after my friend briefly interrupted my train of thought with a trivial conversation, I ended up forgetting it. I was back to square-one—once again, my memory had failed me.

There is no doubt that humans are easily distracted and occasionally forget certain ideas, thoughts, and memories. Sometimes this can be a good thing, such as when we forget painful and traumatic memories. However, we also lose many great ideas that could have benefited us and the world. Clearly, we live in a busy world, filled with many distractions, and thus it is easy for us to be forgetful. But this is no good excuse. Whenever you have a great idea in your head, act like some of the world's greatest thinkers and write them down before you lose them forever. Our unique ideas are some of our greatest possessions and can change the world. Don't take them for granted.

schema:

body:

- ☐ eat a healthy breakfast.
- ☐ take multivitamins.
- ☐ eat lots of yogurt.
- ☐ go for a jog.
- ☐ play with friends and family.

mind:

- ☐ relax with music.
- ☐ take a mental vacation.

goals:

- ☐ :
- ☐ :
- ☐ :

reflections:

day seventy - three:
disjoin the crowd

No one gossips about other people's secret virtues.
Bertrand Russell (1872 - 1970)

Fraternities and sororities are an integral part of life on most college campuses, and most of these organizations were established to install a sense of pride, leadership, and excellence in their members. However, nowadays some of these organizations have replaced old values with excessive drinking and partying. Although I was never a member of any fraternity, I had the opportunity to learn about fraternities and sororities from friends and acquaintances who were pledged members. I learned that several of these people joined, not because they truly believed in the organization, but out of peer-pressure and because they wanted to be recognized as members of a particular group.

It's particularly sad to realize that many of us are so terrified of being by ourselves that we're willing to sacrifice our beliefs and convictions for acceptance by people with dissimilar views. Why should anyone abandon him or herself in exchange for acceptance? There's no doubt that we sometimes get criticized or mocked by other people because of our differences. However, being different isn't always a bad thing. For instance, if all the world's great thinkers, like Einstein and Marie-Curie, were scared of their erratically different ideas, we will not have the great technologies of today. Don't be an automaton in the crowd who is incapable of reason. Be yourself, think logically, express your individuality, and don't join a group because everyone is joining. Only join if you will be yourself or if you want to make a contribution to help other people. Always allow "you" to shine.

schema:

body:
- ☐ eat a healthy breakfast.
- ☐ take multivitamins.
- ☐ drink lots of water.
- ☐ cook a delicious meal.
- ☐ complete several squats.

mind:
- ☐ be kind to everyone.
- ☐ talk less and listen more.

goals:
- ☐ :
- ☐ :
- ☐ :

reflections:

day seventy - four:
point of reference

Civilizations in decline are consistently characterised by a tendency towards standardization and uniformity.
Arnold Toynbee (1889 - 1975)

I am a good freestyle cook, capable of making tasty concoctions of food that are irreproducible. One day, I decided to make an Asian dish with instructions from a cookbook, and after about an hour in the kitchen, the dish looked pretty tasty. However, as soon as I took a bite I knew that something was amiss. The dish tasted nothing like a similar one I enjoyed in a Chinese restaurant. I was confident that I had followed the instructions correctly but soon realized that I had measured one of the ingredients in pints rather than in ounces.

We all know that certain physical properties can be measured with different units. For example, weight can be measured in "pounds" or "grams," and height can be measured in "feet" or "meters." Of course, mistakes will always result if, as I did when cooking, we use the wrong units to measure something. Similarly, many of us get disappointed in life because we measure the level of our success with the wrong measurements. If you ever feel like you are lagging behind in life, make sure that you are using a correct measure of your success. You could easily use a wrong measure, such as making comparisons of your life with the lives of doctors, celebrities, or other highly successful people. Never compare yourself with people who have already climbed to the top! If you do, then you will feel inadequate. In fact, comparing your life with the lives of anyone, regardless of their success, is meaningless because no two people are the same. A great measure of your success will be to set realistic goals for yourself and to see how close you come to accomplishing them.

schema:

body:
- ☐ eat a healthy breakfast.
- ☐ take multivitamins.
- ☐ eat lots of seafood.
- ☐ go for a walk.
- ☐ complete several calf-raises.

mind:
- ☐ be proactive.
- ☐ smile and greet everyone.

goals:
- ☐ :
- ☐ :
- ☐ :

reflections:

day seventy - five:
great responsibilities

Nearly all men can stand adversity, but if you want to test a man's character, give him power.
Abraham Lincoln (1809 - 1865)

As a kid, I loved reading comic books about superheroes because I was astonished by the great powers that these superheroes possessed. Sometimes, I would even imagine myself as a superhero, flying around the world and defeating evil. I became so engulfed by the comic characters that I would get upset whenever the darker sides of the superheroes were revealed to the readers. Back then, I used to think that it was impossible for a lifesaving superhero to have a dark side. However, as I got older I began to understand the poisonous effects of power and how it can corrupt virtuous minds.

Great power is like a kitchen knife—both should be used with great care but, in the wrong hands, can be used for evil. It's unarguable that great power can corrupt the mind. Take a look at all power-drunken world leaders who, although initially starting off as good people, committed unimaginable atrocities to their own people or others. Just like the superheroes in comic books, every one has been bestowed with great talents to benefit humanity. Sadly, many of us never get to develop these talents because we don't discover them or we fear the great responsibilities that come with talents. Don't let your abilities go to waste—take charge and let your talents positively impact the world. However, beware of the intoxicating effects of great talent and power. Always remain humble and virtuous.

schema:

body:
- ☐ eat a healthy breakfast.
- ☐ take multivitamins.
- ☐ eat lots of steamed vegetables.
- ☐ complete several push-ups.
- ☐ complete several sit-ups.

mind:
- ☐ compliment your others.
- ☐ cherish today like it's your last.

goals:
- ☐ :
- ☐ :
- ☐ :

reflections:

day seventy - six:
<u>braggadocio</u>

Self-respect is the cornerstone of all virtue.
John Herschel (1792 - 1871)

Kids are usually very fond of their parents and are quick to brag about them. Once, I saw two boys in the park argue for several minutes about whose father was stronger. From their intense facial and body expressions, I clearly could tell that the boys were both proud of their fathers' strength. However, as an adult I couldn't see the point in their argument. Funny enough, many of us still act like children and brag unnecessarily about such things as our jobs and several worldly possessions. Of course, it is normal for us to sometimes talk about new purchases or gifts, but, if someone does this excessively, then it becomes obnoxious.

Whenever I see adults bragging about their jobs and material possessions, I often wonder if their arguments are in any way valid. For instance, can a professional golfer claim to be a better athlete than a professional football player? Clearly, both sports require different types of athletic abilities. Similarly, every one of us has unique abilities that help society. For this reason, our society needs every profession to function optimally. Don't be sad that your job doesn't sound as prestigious as, say, a scientist or a researcher. If our society only had so-called prestigious professions, then it's very likely that society will crumble. Take pride in whatever you do, but don't become vain because vanity could lead to your downfall or contribute to society's breakdown.

schema:

body:
- ☐ eat a healthy breakfast.
- ☐ take multivitamins.
- ☐ drink lots of water.
- ☐ go for a jog.
- ☐ play with friends and family.

mind:
- ☐ appreciate your body.
- ☐ meditate.

goals:
- ☐ :
- ☐ :
- ☐ :

reflections:

day seventy - seven:
prejudiced bunch

The greatest of faults, I should say, is to be conscious of none.
Thomas Carlyle (1795 - 1881)

In one of my psychology classes as an undergraduate, there was a woman who sat in the front and consistently interrupted the professor with questions about such things as the weather and the professor's fashion sense. Overtime, her behavior began to irritate other students to the point that some students would laugh scornfully whenever she spoke. However, all of this changed when the woman told the entire class her touching story. She had been involved in a terrible car accident that had damaged her brain and left her with severe memory loss and the inability to control her thoughts. As a result, she would blurt out most ideas in her head. She told the class about the pains of rehabilitation and how she was fighting to be normal again. Surprisingly, after her emotional speech several students walked up to her and apologized for their prior rudeness and ignorance of her condition.

Undoubtedly, many of us criticize other people's actions and behaviors, especially when they seem erratic to us. Just like those students who criticized my classmate, many of us are usually ignorant of the condition that we're so quick to judge and criticize. Who are we to judge a person without truly knowing them? This doesn't mean that malicious behaviors should be excused because we don't understand the mind of the perpetrator, but it means that we should be more objective rather than subjective towards others. Sometimes, we might be right in our initial perceptions, but at times we are also wrong. Don't be an ignorant person who is quick to point out other's faults. Be tolerant, considerate, and wary of your criticisms.

schema:

body:
- ☐ eat a healthy breakfast.
- ☐ take multivitamins.
- ☐ eat lots of fresh salad.
- ☐ complete several sit-ups.
- ☐ complete several bench dips.

mind:
- ☐ smile and greet everyone.
- ☐ take a mental vacation.

goals:
- ☐ :
- ☐ :
- ☐ :

reflections:

day seventy - eight:
<u>visualizing</u>

Imagination is more important than knowledge...
Albert Einstein (1879 - 1955)

As a child, remember when it was close to your birthday and you wished that your parents would get you all the toys that you wanted? Of course, most of us had this wish. We would even "unintentionally" express our desires to our parents by, for instance, talking about the toys everyday, drawing pictures of the toys on the wall, and even screaming every time we see the toys on the television. Amazingly, like the laws of magnetism, our parents were compelled (probably out of frustration) to buy at least some of those toys for us. Clearly, as children we could easily visualize our goals and take the necessary steps to achieve them. How come, as we get older and become adults, we forget about or fail to use this ability to be successful?

Visualization is a powerful mental tool. If you doubt the power of visualization, then just think about how much we have accomplished since the Stone Age. If we lacked the ability to visualize, then we will not have all the incredible inventions of today, such as cars, houses, airplanes, and computers. Even cooking a simple meal in the kitchen, like scrambled eggs, requires visualization. Most successful people in the world became successful because of their ability to visualize success and how to obtain it. We all have this amazing ability, and it's unfortunate that many of us don't use it to our full potential. Tap into your ability to visualize the world you desire, and in no time, those thoughts of yours will most likely become reality.

schema:

body:

- ☐ eat a healthy breakfast.
- ☐ take multivitamins.
- ☐ drink lots of fresh juice.
- ☐ complete several bicep curls.
- ☐ complete several squats.

mind:

- ☐ visualize a successful day.
- ☐ prioritize your life.

goals:

- ☐ :
- ☐ :
- ☐ :

reflections:

day seventy - nine:
good people

It is pretty hard to tell what does bring happiness; poverty and wealth have both failed.
Kin Hubbard (1868 - 1930)

One day, I was talking to a friend of mine and he told me that he was depressed because he felt the world was filled with much hate and very little inspiration. I disagreed with his extreme view of the world and tried to help him think more positively. Nevertheless, I understood that his sadness was distorting his perception of life. Clearly, we live in a society that has its share of vindictive people who are out to hurt others. However, as I told my friend, society is also filled with kindhearted people who are out to help others.

Our world is a beautiful place with so many sources of inspiration. However, many of us fail to notice them because we are in the habit of thinking that sources of inspiration have to be grand in nature. Just take a look at nice people, the dogs, birds, blue sky, intricate buildings, and sleek cars. Are not many sources of inspiration very simple? The simple fact that humans, from scratch, designed and built all the existing technologies that we currently enjoy is inspirational. Every human-being can be a living inspiration. Find inspiration in yourself, use your talents to inspire others, and you will be surprised to find that the more you inspire others, the more inspired you will become.

schema:

body:
- ☐ eat a healthy breakfast.
- ☐ take multivitamins.
- ☐ eat some chocolate.
- ☐ stretch several times.
- ☐ complete several shoulder presses.

mind:
- ☐ relax with music.
- ☐ breathe and introspect

goals:
- ☐ :
- ☐ :
- ☐ :

reflections:

day eighty:
the human puzzle

So long as we live among men, let us cherish humanity.
  Andre Gide (1869 - 1951)

In college, I used to be a resident assistant (RA), and I was responsible for the upkeep and maintenance of a floor in one of the residential halls. Every school year, RAs had to attend an obstacle course off of the campus to help build an atmosphere of teamwork. Activities at the obstacle course included races, rock climbing, and a game that involved the formation of a human crossword puzzle. In this puzzle game, every participant was assigned a letter of the alphabet and had to fit in somewhere to complete the answer to a question. During the first time I played, I was amazed by how fast we all scrambled around and found our correct positions, although there were several personality clashes.

As in this game, we all, in the large picture of life, fit together like a complex jigsaw puzzle, and every one of us, in a unique way, is required to make a contribution to the lives of others. It's a shame that many of us are quick to discriminate against others simply because we feel they are inferior to us. All of us are important and are needed for a functioning society. Can you have one part of a car engine—like the pistons or the transmission—without the other parts? No way! We are like the words in a great poem—removing a single word throws everything off. Thus, don't discriminate against others. Always remember that you and everyone else are equally important.

schema:

body:
- ☐ eat a healthy breakfast.
- ☐ take multivitamins.
- ☐ eat lots of yogurt.
- ☐ complete several push-ups.
- ☐ complete several sit-ups.

mind:
- ☐ appreciate your body.
- ☐ cherish today like it's your last.

goals:
- ☐ :
- ☐ :
- ☐ :

reflections:

epoch eight:
isochronal reflections (1)

epoch eight:
isochronal reflections (2)

day eighty - one:
<u>mindless zombies</u>

I have never met a man so ignorant that I couldn't learn
something from him.
Galileo Galilei (1564 - 1642)

One time my friends and I watched a horror movie about
zombies taking over the world and consequently preying on
humans for food. My friends were terrified of the zombies, but I
chuckled or laughed loudly when they came onto the screen. I
find zombie movies very comical—not scary. This may be
because I have seen so many terrible zombie movies over the
years. Nevertheless, it was interesting how my friends and I
reacted differently to the same movie. How could they be
frightened by actors and actresses who wore rags and lots of
makeup?

Of course, we are all different and can have a wide range of
emotions. Rarely do we all feel or act the same in a given
situation. For instance, some people weep with the loss of a
loved one and some people don't. Nonetheless, many of us still
act oblivious to this fact and become upset when others don't
act or react similarly to ourselves. We can't force others to be
like ourselves—this is impossible! If everyone acted and
responded similarly, then we will all be like zombies in those
zombie movies, incapable of reason and driven by the same
impulses. Don't be like one of those mindless zombies whose sole
purpose, if any, is to change everyone to zombies as well. Learn
from other people's differences and use those differences to
better understand your own uniqueness.

---

schema:

body:
- ☐ eat a healthy breakfast.
- ☐ take multivitamins.
- ☐ drink lots of water.
- ☐ complete several standing rows.
- ☐ complete several calf-raises.

mind:
- ☐ prioritize your life.
- ☐ appreciate nature.

goals:
- ☐ :
- ☐ :
- ☐ :

reflections:

day eighty - two:
<u>the scornful</u>

Envy is the ulcer of the soul.
   Socrates (469 BC - 399 BC)

Obviously, the world is a diverse collection of people with different traits, personalities, talents and ideas. Therefore, it is not surprising that two people can have opposite views and opinions on the same issue. For example, an optimist will say that the world is at least half filled with good people who truly care about others, and a pessimist will say that the majority of the world is filled with bad people who are compelled to hurt others. Nevertheless, which of these views is more accurate? The truth of either view seems impossible to prove.

One thing in the world, however, is much easier to prove and that is the existence of moral truths. The fact that there are certain acts that we all agree are evil, such as rape and genocide, means that there are moral truths. One person might view a deed as good, and someone else might view that deed as evil, but this is not to say that both people are right. Sadly, some people have become so engulfed with hatred that they allow it to control their lives and shroud their ability to recognize moral truths. Hatred is like a deep cut on a leg! If cleaned quickly and properly will heal but if left untreated will become infected. Having hatred for other people results in self-hatred, and this often leads to self destruction. Never let any kind of hatred control your life and transform you from a kindhearted person into a person who acts without a conscience. Practice compassion, be nice to others, and stay clear of hateful people.

schema:

body:
- ☐ eat a healthy breakfast.
- ☐ take multivitamins.
- ☐ eat lots of fruits.
- ☐ go for a jog.
- ☐ complete bicep curls.

mind:
- ☐ practice tolerance.
- ☐ smile and greet everyone today.

goals:
- ☐ :
- ☐ :
- ☐ :

reflections:

day eighty - three:
<u>the masterpiece</u>

Small opportunities are often the beginning of great enterprises.
Demosthenes (384 BC - 322 BC)

My father, besides being a surgeon, loved to draw people and animals. As a young chap, I enjoyed watching him draw and listening to him talk about great artists like Leonardo da Vinci, Botticelli, and Pablo Picasso, and how these artists used their imaginations and skills to produce great works of art. My father said that anyone can learn to draw well, just like anyone can learn the principles of good writing. I know that, to a large extent, my father was correct. If every one of us practiced drawing everyday and developed our imaginations, it's undeniable that the world will be filled with many more artists.

Practice may not always make perfect, but we should strive to become great at what we pursue. This usually requires us to use our imaginations, which, unfortunately, many of us don't realize. The difference between an artist and a great artist can often be imaginative powers. Say two artists of equal talent were given the same paints and brushes and told to paint the same scene outside a window. It's unlikely that both artists would paint identical pictures—the quality of the paintings would largely be dependent upon the imagination of the artists. Similarly, many of us are given opportunities to succeed in life, and, like the artists, our chances of coming out on top are often dependent upon our imaginations and persistence. Don't take life for granted. Seize every opportunity and use it to produce historic masterpieces, like those of da Vinci.

schema:

body:

- ☐ eat a healthy breakfast.
- ☐ take multivitamins.
- ☐ eat lots of fresh fish.
- ☐ stretch several times.
- ☐ complete several lunges.

mind:

- ☐ be patient.
- ☐ prioritize your life.

goals:

- ☐ :
- ☐ :
- ☐ :

reflections:

day eighty - four:
party planners

Everything you can imagine is real.
Pablo Picasso (1881 - 1973)

Occasionally, I like to have friends over to have a nice gathering. Anyone who has ever hosted a party should know that proper planning is required for a successful event. I have come to realize that there is a big similarity between how we organize parties and how other people in our society strive to help us attain and accomplish our goals. Just as when you take the initiative to go to college and your state government gives you grants or scholarships, every time I propose the idea of having a party with my friends they help make the party a reality by doing things like calling people and buying food.

Interestingly, many of us are ignorant about the fact that our ideas and actions have the power to influence and compel others into helping us accomplish our goals. If we really want to achieve our goals and we actively think about them, then our thoughts will eventually help make paths for us to achieve our goals. Sadly, many of us never do this, and consequently never get to execute or accomplish our goals. Don't keep your goals locked up in your head! Our ideas are like perfume scents that, when sprayed, catch people's attention. Never waste your ideas or goals. Instead, begin to actively ponder and act on them. You will be amazed that other people, including strangers, will start working eagerly to help you.

schema:

body:
- ☐ eat a healthy breakfast.
- ☐ take multivitamins.
- ☐ eat lots of seafood.
- ☐ complete several sit-ups.
- ☐ complete several shoulder presses.

mind:
- ☐ talk less and listen more.
- ☐ laugh at every chance.

goals:
- ☐ :
- ☐ :
- ☐ :

reflections:

day eighty - five:
unlimited desire

Prediction is very difficult, especially about the future.
Niels Bohr (1885 - 1962)

When I was younger, I escorted my parents to a buffet lunch at an elegant hotel. I remember becoming so excited when I saw all the food that I immediately dashed towards the table to literally eat all that I could eat. However, I was stopped by my mother, who had decided to ration my portions. As she walked around the table filling my plate, my eyes drifted to a tasty looking shrimp dish, and I begged my mother for a taste. Although she sternly refused my request, I was grateful to her later on because most people at the buffet, including my dad, got terribly sick from the shrimp

It is normal for us to become upset when we don't get the things we want— I know I did with the shrimp. Nevertheless, many of us don't realize that some of our missed opportunities in life have been life savers. For instance, some of us are upset because we have not gotten those motorcycles or sport cars we always have wanted, and this has probably saved our health or even lives. However, because we never get physically hurt, many of us never realize how those missed opportunities saved our lives. Let's be honest with ourselves! Disappointments can be a real bummer, but many of them can also be blessings in disguise. Next time, when you are disappointed or upset about missed opportunities, just keep this in mind—your life might have been a lot worse.

schema:

body:
- ☐ eat a healthy breakfast.
- ☐ take multivitamins.
- ☐ drink lots of water.
- ☐ complete several push-ups.
- ☐ complete several lunges.

mind:
- ☐ inspire others.
- ☐ prioritize your life.

goals:
- ☐ :
- ☐ :
- ☐ :

reflections:

Olusegun 'Sheg' Aranmolate

day eighty - six:
emotion detectives

Feel the fear and do it anyway.
Susan Jeffers (1942 - ****)

Dogs are great human companions and are very capable of learning. When watching cop shows on the television, I always find it fascinating to watch police dogs take down criminals and smell narcotics in the strangest hiding places. Obviously, dogs have a sense of smell that is much greater than that of humans, and as a result dogs can recognize several odors that we can't. I have even heard that some dogs' sense of smell is so great that they can smell human emotions such as love, compassion, hatred, confidence, and fear.

Although we don't rely on our noses, humans are similar to dogs in that we can sense or predict other people's emotions—we can tell when they are sad, happy, or nervous. Many of us, however, forget the fact that the way we perceive ourselves strongly determines the way others perceive us. For example, if you act unkindly towards others then many of them will view and treat you as an unkind person. Similarly, if you act and speak confidently towards others then they will likely view and treat you as secure rather than as an insecure person. Sadly, people with low self-esteem are often taken advantage of by others who sense their insecurities and who exploit their weaknesses. Don't let others take advantage of you because you're radiating fear. Change your perception and change your world.

schema:

body:
- ☐ eat a healthy breakfast.
- ☐ take multivitamins.
- ☐ eat lots of fruits.
- ☐ get a massage.
- ☐ take a walk.

mind:
- ☐ be kind to everyone.
- ☐ smile and greet everyone.

goals:
- ☐ :
- ☐ :
- ☐ :

reflections:

day eighty - seven:
<u>impenitent</u>

The most perfidious way of harming a cause consists of defending it deliberately with faulty arguments.
Friedrich Nietzsche (1844 - 1900)

Once, I was shopping for a pair of jeans in the mall when a family of five walked into the store. As soon as the parents began shopping, the kids started running around and screaming. The kids even knocked down one of the store mannequins, and instead of acknowledging their mess, they continued with their ruckus. Their parents were obviously embarrassed and, after picking up the mannequin, scolded their kids. But the kids surprisingly refused to apologize to the store clerk and the family left the store in embarrassment.

Unruly kids in public can be bothersome, and many of us get irritated by these kids, especially when they are unapologetic for their disruptive behaviors. Nevertheless, we must realize that kids learn their behavior from older individuals around them and that includes being unapologetic. Accordingly, we all must be better examples to younger people and learn to apologize when wrong. Never feel that apologizing or admitting your mistakes makes you look weak or foolish. In fact, doing this makes us more respectable because the act of apologizing requires humility and courage. It takes more effort to refuse to apologize or to try and rationalize our bad actions. Don't be a fool who refuses to apologize to others like those boisterous children in the store. Mend your bad ways!

schema:

body:

- ☐ eat a healthy breakfast.
- ☐ take multivitamins.
- ☐ eat some chocolate.
- ☐ complete several sit-ups.
- ☐ complete several squats.

mind:

- ☐ visualize your wonderful day.
- ☐ smile and greet everyone today.

goals:

- ☐ :
- ☐ :
- ☐ :

reflections:

Olusegun 'Sheg' Aranmolate

day eighty - eight:
the latent flames

Hate no one; hate their vices, not themselves.
J. G. C. Brainard (1796 - 1828)

I will never forget the excitement I felt when I moved from my restrictive dorm room to my own apartment. However, this occurred in the summer and my new apartment lacked air conditioning, so I soon wished I was back in my air-conditioned dorm room. One evening the heat became so unbearable that I called a service technician for help. After inspecting my apartment, the technician informed me that the intense heat was due to the summer heat in combination with the heat emitted from the natural gas heating unit, which was designed to continuously burn at a low level.

After finding out this news that I would be cooped up in a heat trap all summer, I became very angry at my landlord, who never informed me of the heating problem. Nevertheless, it was a learning experience because, after a while, I learned how to control my anger and to control myself from projecting my frustrations on others. Our anger can be like the flames of the heating unit, which lay dim until fueled with more propane. Just like heating units have thermostats that control flame levels, we have the ability to control the levels of our anger. Think of the consequences of acting on your anger and let this be a guide for your anger control. Never let your anger explode uncontrollably.

schema:

body:
- ☐ eat a healthy breakfast.
- ☐ take multivitamins.
- ☐ drink lots of juice.
- ☐ stretch several times.
- ☐ go for a walk.

mind:
- ☐ think positively.
- ☐ take a mental vacation.

goals:
- ☐ :
- ☐ :
- ☐ :

reflections:

day eighty - nine:
seeking attention

The joy of a spirit is the measure of its power.
Ninon de Lenclos (1620 - 1705)

While I was in college, I worked as a valet parker near Washington, D.C., and had the opportunity to drive the cars of several senators and business executives. It was fun because I got to drive several expensive cars and, at the same time, learn about the correlation between flashy cars and flashy people. I noticed that many people with expensive cars loved to brag and usually cared more about their cars than about the valet parkers. Many of us buy expensive cars for the luxury features and for the attention that such cars attract. Consequently, many of us, when we see an expensive car, assume that the owner is very affluent. However, this isn't always the case because many people who are in serious debt drive expensive cars for the craved attention.

Humans love attention and this is shown in the way we dress, talk, and act. Unfortunately, many of us have become so engulfed by our materialistic society that we feel that we can't be noticed by others until we own the latest clothes, gadgets, and gizmos. However, we must realize that we don't need to have all the new stuff to be noticed by others. What ever happened to sharing a genuine smile, nice gestures, or a hearty laugh with someone? These beautiful manners are what really get us noticed. You can own the best attires, but if you don't have a good attitude to complement it, then you blend in with the superficial world. A beautiful smile and good gesture are like new jewelries that sparkle in the light. Be genuine and sparkle with your gleaming smile and great attitude. This will get you all the positive attention that you desire.

schema:

body:

- ☐ eat a healthy breakfast.
- ☐ take multivitamins.
- ☐ eat lots of fresh salad.
- ☐ cook a delicious meal.
- ☐ get a massage.

mind:

- ☐ practice tolerance.
- ☐ smile and greet everyone today.

goals:

- ☐ :
- ☐ :
- ☐ :

reflections:

day ninety:
right directions

The best way to predict the future is to invent it.
Alan Kay (1940 - ****)

A few years ago, drivers had to rely on maps on paper to get directions. Nowadays, we can use online maps to get directions in seconds. With the emergence of the internet and Global Positioning System (GPS) technology, paper maps have almost become obsolete. Why do all the work involved in reading a paper map when, with a few strokes on a computer keyboard, you can get all the directions you need? However, even with all this modern help, many of us still get lost on trips because no computer can prevent us from making wrong turns and no online map is perfect, at least presently.

Our journey through life can be similar to driving in traffic with online directions and just as many of us can be overly confident in relying on online directions to get us places, we can be overly confident in the direction that our lives are going. In pursuing our goals, we can take wrong turns or get distracted by other people, things or situations and end up in unplanned destinations. The world is filled with several variables and sometimes our choices become unintentionally altered. However, it's important to self reflect periodically to make sure that you are where you want to be in life. As with following online directions, don't be afraid to stop and ask other people for guidance or to trust your own instincts.

schema:

body:

- ☐ eat a healthy breakfast.
- ☐ take multivitamins.
- ☐ eat lots of yogurt.
- ☐ complete several push-ups.
- ☐ complete several sit-ups.

mind:

- ☐ breathe and introspect.
- ☐ appreciate your day.

goals:

- ☐ :
- ☐ :
- ☐ :

reflections:

epoch nine:
isochronal reflections (1)

epoch nine:
<u>isochronal reflections (2)</u>

day ninety - one:
similar happiness

If you want others to be happy, practice compassion. If you want to be happy, practice compassion.
Tenzin Gyatso (1935 - ****)

When I was a young boy, every morning my dog Murphy accompanied me on my way to school. When I would near the school entrance, he would begin to whine in sadness, and when I would arrive home later on, he would wag his tail and bark with excitement. Surely, many of us experience or have experienced this with our dogs. It is obvious that our dogs enjoy our presence, but can we know with certainty that our dogs experience happiness? Whatever excitement Murphy felt was genuine and it made me feel happy about myself, but since dogs cannot speak human languages, I will never know about the emotions, if any, that he truly felt.

What I do know is that all humans are capable of experiencing happiness. Some people say that it can be difficult to find reasons in life to be happy. If an alien from a different planet asked you to explain happiness and to give ten reasons why you should be happy, will you be able to give an answer? I personally will be unable to provide a full answer, but I will say that, to become happy, we must identify the keys to happiness, such as being kind, compassionate, selfless, and humble, and we must pursue these keys. Happiness is like any sport that requires constant practice for proficiency. Thus, the more you pursue and use the keys of happiness, the greater the odds that you will experience happiness. Pursue those keys today!

schema:

body:

- ☐ eat a healthy breakfast.
- ☐ take multivitamins.
- ☐ eat some of chocolate.
- ☐ stretch several times.
- ☐ dance whenever you can.

mind:

- ☐ think positively.
- ☐ laugh at every chance.

goals:

- ☐ :
- ☐ :
- ☐ :

reflections:

Olusegun 'Sheg' Aranmolate

day ninety - two:
<u>vaulted memories</u>

One must have a good memory to be able to keep the promises one makes.
Friedrich Nietzsche (1844 - 1900)

When we meet people for the first time, we usually shake their hand and say our names. This may seem like a simple gesture, but this gesture involves many complicated mental and physical processes. For instance, when we meet someone we remember his or her face, the circumstances of the meeting, other people who were present, and, if we are lucky, we remember his or her name. The ability to form memories is clearly a large part of life, and it's not an exaggeration to conclude that the human experience is based on our interaction with previously acquired precious memories—good and bad memories.

Our memories are like files in a file cabinet that are ready for us to retrieve. On a daily basis, there are moments when we can't recall memories or parts of memories. These moments can be frustrating, especially when you know that the memory or part of the memory was a good one. Even though this can happen to anyone, many of us are quick to get annoyed or angry with people who have severe memory loss. However, just like we are all susceptible to catching the same diseases, all of us are susceptible to someday experiencing severe memory loss. You can never know what it feels like to be another person, so we should tolerate other people's afflictions to make them feel better. Don't treat such people poorly—instead, give them new pleasurable memories.

schema:

body:
- ☐ eat a healthy breakfast.
- ☐ take multivitamins.
- ☐ drink lots of water.
- ☐ go for a jog.
- ☐ complete several shoulder presses.

mind:
- ☐ compliment others.
- ☐ inspire others.

goals:
- ☐ :
- ☐ :
- ☐ :

reflections:

day ninety - three:
reinforcement

The goal of life is living in agreement with nature.
    Zeno (335 BC - 264 BC)

Humans love fashion, and this is quite evident by the large number of magazines dedicated to designer clothes. Every season, many of us browse and study fashion magazines like studious students who are searching for the world's next greatest invention. As a result we tend to be very knowledgeable of what's in and what's out.   Aside from "fashionability," few people truly appreciate the value of clothes. Have you ever noticed how clothes are made from a bunch of flimsy threads? It's amazing how all those threads can entwine together to make a sturdy piece of clothing.

A single cotton thread will break with the slightest force, so how come, say, jeans, which are made entirely from cotton, are so durable?   To put it simply, all the threads add their individual strengths together. Similarly, many little ideas can combine to make great works for society.   Think of all the books, scientific experiments, and buildings that came about after people shared ideas. Every one of us has unique ideas that are capable of influencing and changing the world. Unfortunately, though, many of these ideas (like a single cotton thread) are lost because we never share them with other people. Learn about other people's ideas and share your own ideas with others. Your ideas could be great by themselves or could help someone else make a great discovery. Always remember that a great mind along with its idea is terrible thing to waste.

schema:

body:
- ☐ eat a healthy breakfast.
- ☐ take multivitamins.
- ☐ eat lots of fruits.
- ☐ complete several sit-ups.
- ☐ complete several calf-raises.

mind:
- ☐ relax to music.
- ☐ prioritize your life.

goals:
- ☐ :
- ☐ :
- ☐ :

reflections:

day ninety - four:
navigation system

You always pass failure on the way to success.
Mickey Rooney (1920 - ****)

Have you ever been lost when driving someplace? It can be a harrowing experience. Once, I drove to visit a friend and, after it started pouring down rain and a few wrong turns, I became completely lost. I kept on driving in hopes that I would find the right road but it never came. Luckily, I found a gas station along the way and asked the sales clerk for assistance, and to my relief I discovered that I was only about a mile from my friend's house.

The feeling of being lost in life can be overwhelming to the point that we feel like we are trapped in a maze. However, remaining calm during these times can save unneeded stress. Even wild animals have methods to navigate through dense woods, so we should use our internal sense of direction (besides online maps!) to ensure that we're able to avoid getting lost. This may require goal-setting and studying "maps" of the areas in life that you will like to explore so that you understand the "big picture." Everyone has this internal sense of direction—we just have to develop it. Keep your cool and you'll find your self where you want to be.

schema:

body:
- ☐ eat a healthy breakfast.
- ☐ take multivitamins.
- ☐ eat lots of fresh salad.
- ☐ go for a walk.
- ☐ stretch several times.

mind:
- ☐ compliment your colleagues.
- ☐ take a mental vacation.

goals:
- ☐ :
- ☐ :
- ☐ :

reflections:

day ninety - five:
<u>flexible</u>

Adapt or perish, now as ever, is nature's inexorable imperative.
H. G. Wells (1866 - 1946)

We live in an ever-changing world of technologies, fashions, and politics, and this requires us to constantly adapt. Once, I saw a movie about a young man who had been sleeping for countless years in a cryogenic chamber, only to be awoken by a couple curious boys. The movie had a romantic storyline that suggested that certain human emotions like affection, kindness, and love are timeless. But the man had to adjust to an entirely different society filled with such changes as new modes of transportation, new infrastructures, and new medicines. Can you imagine such drastic changes?

Of course, change can often be a nice experience. However, many of us get frustrated and sometimes depressed following drastic changes in our lives. For instance, a friend of mine got promoted to a position that he had always wanted only to find out it was a bad fit. With new long hours and a stressful boss, the job made him exhausted and depressed. My friend's story teaches us to be careful about the changes we pursue because we may later regret the changes. Nevertheless, we all need to be flexible enough to change but resilient enough to withstand the effects of change.

schema:

body:
- ☐ eat a healthy breakfast.
- ☐ take multivitamins.
- ☐ eat some chocolate.
- ☐ dance whenever you can.
- ☐ get a massage.

mind:
- ☐ apologize for your faults.
- ☐ meditate.

goals:
- ☐ :
- ☐ :
- ☐ :

reflections:

day ninety - six:
impenetrable thoughts

Any fool can criticize, condemn, and complain - and most fools do.
Dale Carnegie (1888 - 1955)

Once, I saw a TV show about a street savvy magician. I was immediately intrigued because, as a kid, I was fond of Harry Houdini, a great magician, and I thought magic was real. Of course, as I got older I came to the bitter realization that magical acts were simply illusions resulting from our flawed sensory system (our perception). Nevertheless, I watched the show to see if I could figure out the "prestige" behind his acts and was immediately impressed by the novelty of his acts, especially when he performed the impossible task of reading other people's thoughts. This trick was amazing because the human mind is like an impenetrable fortress.

We all share some commonality in our flawed perceptions of reality that, under the right conditions and state of mind, we can be deceived into believing things. Have you ever taken a moment to think about the way you think and the factors that influence your thought process? This might seem like a circular question, but the truth is that the way we think determines the way we view the world. Don't let other people trick you into believing anything. If you are in a debate or argument with someone, don't let yourself get dragged into fallacious reasoning, like when people try to convince you that something is true because a majority of people believe it to be true. In particular, don't get caught up in all the talking points of politicians, some of whom can be the greatest illusionists or distorters of the truth.

schema:

body:

- ☐ eat a healthy breakfast.
- ☐ take multivitamins.
- ☐ drink lots of fresh juice.
- ☐ complete several bicep-curls.
- ☐ complete several bench dips.

mind:

- ☐ inspire others to change.
- ☐ breathe and introspect.

goals:

- ☐ :
- ☐ :
- ☐ :

reflections:

Olusegun 'Sheg' Aranmolate

day ninety - seven:
artistic interpretation

Opinions founded on prejudice are always sustained with the greatest of violence.
Francis Jeffrey (1773 - 1850)

The Mona Lisa is one of the most famous paintings by the great artist Leonardo da Vinci, and it depicts a young lady gazing directly at the viewers with a countenance that lacks expression. Despite being a rather boring-looking painting, it has become the subject of much analysis and parody by people from all works of life. There are numerous interpretations of the painting and many believe it has several religious, sexual, and aesthetic overtones. This painting is particularly intriguing to me, not necessarily for its great artistic and aesthetic values, but because it reveals a lot about the way we judge and interpret our lives and the lives of others.

Every one of us has a unique view of life that results from our biology and environment. Just as people have different interpretations of the Mona Lisa, we always have different accounts of the same incident, such as a political debate or basketball game. Because of our subjective nature, many of us are quick to criticize other people's interpretations and impose our subjective views and opinions on others. Sadly, many of us fail to realize that our opinions are sometimes incorrect and, similar to a toddler who clings onto his or her parents, many of us cling to our false opinions. This, however, doesn't mean that we should ever abandon our values, principles, and opinions, but rather be willing to acknowledge the potential validity of other people's opinions.

schema:

body:

- ☐ eat a healthy breakfast.
- ☐ take multivitamins.
- ☐ eat lots of seafood.
- ☐ go for a jog.
- ☐ complete several sit-ups.

mind:

- ☐ practice tolerance.
- ☐ cherish today like it's your last.

goals:

- ☐ :
- ☐ :
- ☐ :

reflections:

day ninety - eight:
knowledgeable criticism

If you are not criticized, you may not be doing much.
Donald H. Rumsfeld (1932 - ****)

I am very particular about the movies I see in the theater because time is scarce and I only want to see great movies. Whenever there is a highly anticipated movie coming to the theater, I read the reviews of the movie from film critics. Movie reviews have rarely convinced me to watch a movie but have given me a sense of the plot. Nevertheless, over the years I have realized that, despite the subjective nature of movie criticisms, there is usually some truth to the critiques.

Criticism is important for our growth and the growth of our society. For example, in the scientific world some of the world's greatest scientific breakthroughs and inventions have resulted from corrections made to previously criticized works (e.g. in the development of the Polio vaccine, which has saved millions of children from Polio). Many of us don't like to be criticized but love to criticize others. It is absurd that many of us are quick to find faults in others when we're blind to our own flaws. We "blind critics" may help others by pointing out their faults but we never improve ourselves. Criticized people usually repair their faults while many of us criticizers are left to wallow in ignorance of our faults. Remember that the Oscar Awards and movie critics help consumers determine the quality of a movie. If there was a similar awards show or group of critiques for your attitudes and behavior, how well will you be rated? Don't be a "blind critic"— it's ok to give constructive criticism of others, just accept correct criticism of yourself.

schema:

body:
- ☐ eat a healthy breakfast.
- ☐ take multivitamins.
- ☐ drink lots of green tea.
- ☐ complete several standing rows.
- ☐ complete several sit-ups.

mind:
- ☐ visualize your successful day.
- ☐ smile and greet everyone today.

goals:
- ☐ :
- ☐ :
- ☐ :

reflections:

day ninety - nine:
the stock exchange

Take calculated risks. That is quite different from being rash.
George S. Patton (1885 - 1945)

My father used to be a member of several medical associations, and every year we would host a couple meetings in our house. These meetings were memorable because my mother would always cook delicious food for our guests and I would patrol the dining room table like a vulture, impatiently waiting for the meetings to be over so that I could feast. As soon as my father's friends began to eat, they would often digress from their conversations about medicine to talk about retirement plans and the stock market. During these conversations, I learned much about the international stock market and even began to follow it on my own.

The course of our lives can be similar to the stock market. For example, just as investors should learn about a company before investing in its stocks, we should best understand our strengths and weaknesses before we pursue our goals in life. Also, similar to investors who make both long and short-term investments, we need to have long and short-term goals in our lives. This helps us maximize our successes and minimize our failures. In addition, just as investors are extremely cautious in putting all their money in one stock option, we should be very cautions in placing all our hope in one goal. We must realize that there's always a risk of failure. Nevertheless, taking calculated risks in life can be the difference between success and failure. Be as knowledgeable as possible about any risks that you take in pursuit of success.

schema:

body:
- ☐ eat a healthy breakfast.
- ☐ take multivitamins.
- ☐ eat lots of fruit.
- ☐ stretch several times.
- ☐ get a massage.

mind:
- ☐ be kind to everyone.
- ☐ laugh at every chance.

goals:
- ☐ :
- ☐ :
- ☐ :

reflections:

day one - hundred:
different kind of genius

The secret to creativity is knowing how to hide your sources.
Albert Einstein (1879 - 1955)

The word Einstein—taken from the name of Albert Einstein, one of the world's greatest physicists—has become synonymous with the word genius. He was a genius, whose scientific works answered some of the most challenging questions in physics and chemistry, such as the relationship between energy and the speed of light. Einstein never limited himself to the sciences and also made profound contributions to the liberal arts and world politics (e.g. denouncing the Nazi movement in Germany and participating in several civil rights movements).   As a child, Einstein had speech impairment and he also failed his first entrance exam into college. However, like most successful people he didn't give up and successfully reapplied.

We live in a world where, for the most part, being different is condemned and conformity is praised. There are many of us who are afraid of our unique characteristics, such as unique ideas and intellectual abilities that we try very hard to blend into the crowd. Have you ever heard the story of the ugly duckling? This duckling was ostracized by other ducks because it looked unordinary—later in life the ugly ducking transformed into a majestic swan. Just like the duckling, there are times when it is impossible for us to blend into the crowd and, during those times, it's important for us to let our differences shine. If great thinkers like Einstein had decided to ignore their unique ideas, then we might not be enjoying many luxuries and technologies. Don't be scared to share your unique characteristics—they may make a lasting contribution to humanity.   At the very least, sharing your uniqueness will bring you happiness and may help people around you.

schema:

body:
- ☐ eat a healthy breakfast.
- ☐ take multivitamins.
- ☐ eat lots of salad.
- ☐ cook a delicious meal.
- ☐ play with friends and family.

mind:
- ☐ appreciate your day.
- ☐ inspire others to change.

goals:
- ☐ :
- ☐ :
- ☐ :

reflections:

epoch ten:
<u>isochronal reflections (1)</u>

epoch ten:
isochronal reflections (2)

the end!

"The end of ONE is the beginning of TWO."
Olusegun 'Sheg' Aranmolate

about the author:

Olusegun 'Sheg' Aranmolate was born on March 26, 1983 in Lagos, Nigeria. He was raised by his father, a renowned British trained plastic surgeon, and his mother, a retired medical radiographer. He is the only son and fourth child of five children. His parents always stressed the value of a good education and hard work, and by age eight, Sheg had already started observing his father at work in his hospital. During those visits, Sheg watched his father help the sick and started developing a strong sense of compassion for the less fortunate. By the young age of twelve, he already had a strong desire to study medicine and become a surgeon like his father.

Olusegun came to the United States in July 2001 at the age of eighteen in pursuit of a college and medical degree. He attended the University of Maryland, Baltimore County (UMBC), where he earned a Bachelors degree in Biochemistry and Molecular Biology and a minor degree in Psychology. After his undergraduate education, he spent another year at UMBC in graduate school, conducting scientific research. He completed his thesis at the age twenty-two and graduated in May 2006 with a Masters degree in Applied Molecular Biology.

Olusegun is a young, well-respected motivational writer and prolific speaker. He is a philanthropist, an activist, a fashion model, the co-founder of the Aranmolate Foundation for Deformed Children, and the founder of the Inspivia, Inc. He considers motivating people his greatest passion in life and continually strives to find fascinating ways to inspire others. His personal experiences and interactions with people as a fitness instructor, a scientist, and a fashion model has enabled him to formulate several unique approaches to life coaching that combines core elements of motivational speaking with the rigor of fitness training. Sheg was one of the top five contestants on the ABC smash hit show, Oprah's Big Give show. He has also been featured in a couple magazines, newspaper articles, and television stations. Olusegun has a strong desire to attend medical school in the future. He is currently based in Nashville, Tennessee.

www.olushegun.com

1916653

Made in the USA